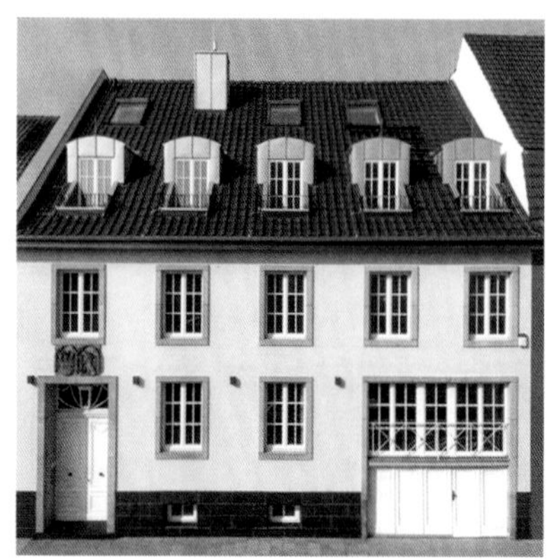

KOPFERMANN-FUHRMANN STIFTUNG

San-Remo-Straße 6, Düsseldorf

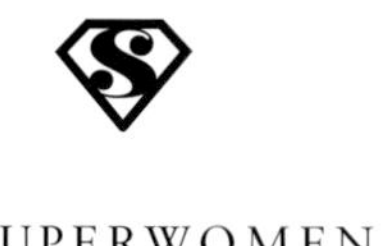

#1_SUPERWOMEN

# JANA SCHRÖDER

*The Early Years*

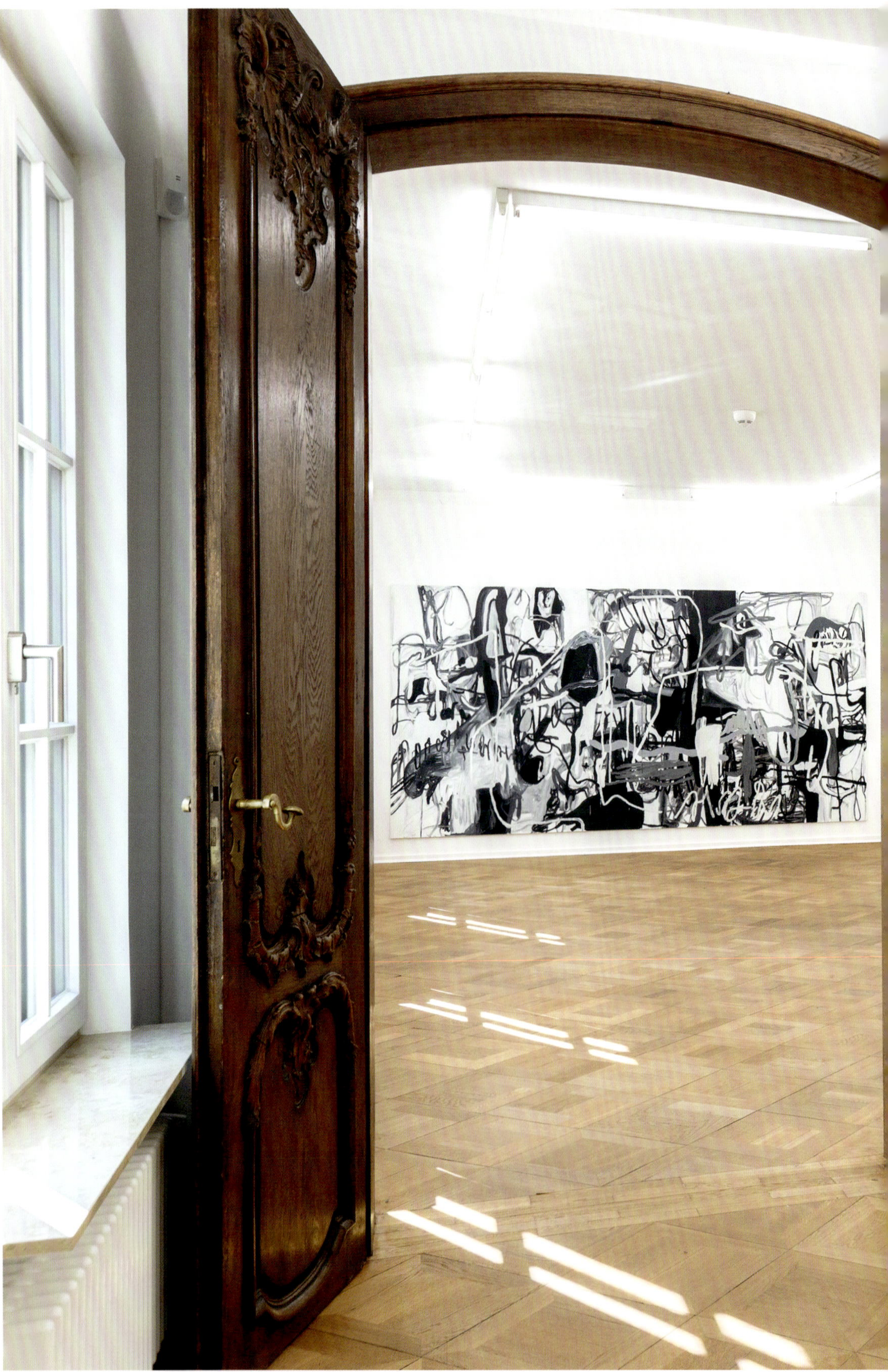

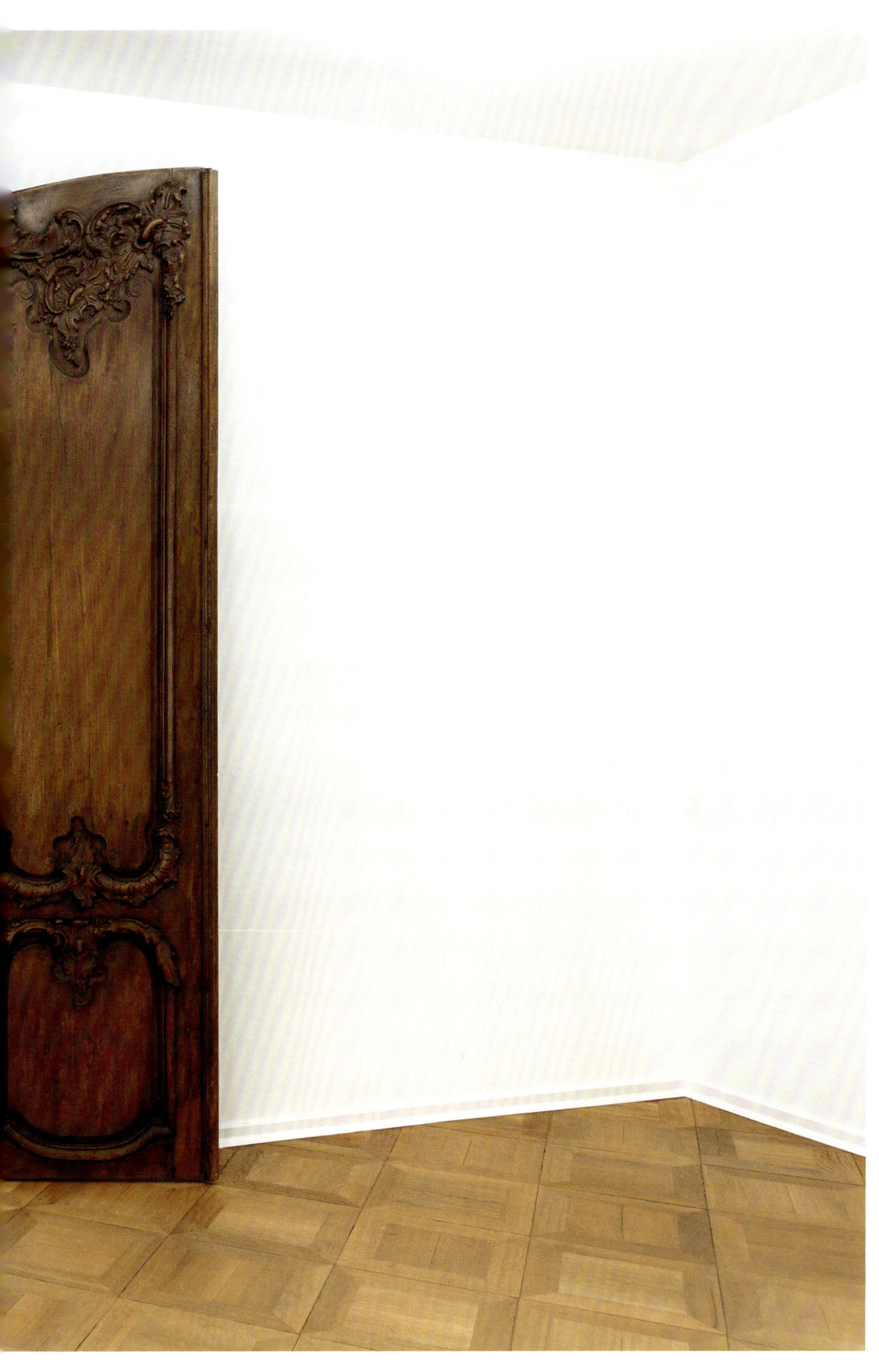

# „Superwomen“

## *Benjamin-Novalis Hofmann*

Mit der Künstlerin Jana Schröder eröffnet der Auftakt einer Ausstellungs-Serie,
die ich für die Kopfermann-Fuhrmann Stiftung als Kurator verantworte.
In loser Folge werden Präsentationen mit Malerinnen der jüngeren Generation
in den Räumen der Stiftung gezeigt.
Den einzelnen künstlerischen Positionen liegt jeweils eine herausragende Idee
von abstrakter Malerei im 21. Jahrhundert zugrunde.
Die einzelnen Künstlerinnen zeichnen sich durch entschiedene Haltung und
große Persönlichkeit aus.
Sigrid Kopfermann würde sie sehr mögen.

– Jana Schröder

Jana Schröder ist eine große Malerin.
Nicht allein durch ihr Gardemaß als großgewachsene Frau freilich,
sondern durch ihr unermüdliches Atelier-Schaffen.
Wohlgemut und mit wehenden Fahnen zieht sie in die Mal-Schlacht,
scheut nicht das Risiko und ist immer auch bereit den Kampf um das
Motiv zu verlieren.
Aufgeben ist keine Option.
Stillstand ebenfalls nicht.

Aufschlag Jana Schröder:
Es wird gemetzelt als gäbe es kein Morgen.
Das Atelier in Eller ein Neonbunker und künstlichem Licht sei Dank ist
das verblassende Tageslicht nicht weiter von Belang.
Kunstlicht und Kinderzimmer, Keller-chique und Material-Chaos,
begonnene Leinwände überall –
von Jana und auch Ihrem Mann Andreas Breunig
brother-in-crime!

Maler-Paar mit Paar Kindern –
Lebensmodell Familie mit kreativem Output
und Stillstand ist keine Option!

Tie break:
Linien-Gewirr und Linien-Gewürm kreuchen über die großformatigen
Leinwände; atemlos keuchend sehen wir dort vor uns
Bild oder Zeichnung?

Gemalte Zeichnung und das Bild –
Oder doch mit Farbe auf Leinwand
gezeichnetes Bild?
Malerei weil mit Pinsel und Farbe?
Das ist naheliegend!

In der Vorstellungswelt Janas ist Alles naheliegend:
Rom liegt neben Los Angeles und Düsseldorf liegt am Jangtse!

Gelblich trüb mäandert der breite Strom, ein Rinnsal freundlich-steingrau
auf der Leinwand – wächst und teilt das Bild:
Links und Rechts
Oben und Unten
Wo beginnt das Bild überhaupt? Haben diese Bilder eigentlich ein
definiertes Ende?
Und wo genau ist oben?
Begrenzt der Bildraum das Bild, oder das Format des Keilrahmens
den Bildraum?

In Jana Schröders Kunst gibt es keine Begrenzung, die Ausdehnung
Ihrer Vorstellungskraft ist unendlich, Supergirl beats!

Die gemalte Zeichnung ist gezeichnete Malerei, das Bild voller
kryptographischer Zeichen eingewoben und seine Farb-Signale verwobenes
Nervenzellen-Geflecht eines autonomen Bildraums 2.0.

Gewürm umschlingt den farb-fingernden Pinsel und ein weiteres Bild erkämpft
seinen Platz im Atelier und emanzipiert sich im Bild-Labyrinth
des Neonbunkers.

Matchball Jana Schröder

# “Superwomen”

## *Benjamin-Novalis Hofmann*

The artist Jana Schröder opens the beginning of a series of exhibitions for the Kopfermann-Fuhrmann Foundation for which I am responsible as curator.
Presentations of the work of women painters of the younger generation are being shown in a loose sequence in the rooms of the foundation.
An outstanding idea of abstract painting in the twenty-first century underlies each of the individual artistic positions.
The individual artists are characterized by a determined attitude and a great personality.
Sigrid Kopfermann would have liked them very much.

– Jana Schröder

Jana Schröder is a painter of great stature.
However, not just due to her dimensions as an adult woman, but by her tireless studio creation. Light-heartedly and with flags flying, she goes into battle with paint, does not shy away from taking risks, and is always prepared to lose the struggle for the motif.
Surrendering is not an option.
Standing still is not an option either.

Jana Schröder’s serve:
Slaughter takes place as if there were no tomorrow.
The studio in Eller a neon bunker and fading daylight is no longer a concern thanks to artificial lighting.
Artificial light and children’s room, cellar-chic and material chaos, started canvases all around—
by Jana as well as her husband, Andreas Breunig,
brother-in-crime!

A painter couple with a couple of children—
A living model of a family with a creative output,
and standing still is not an option!

Tiebreak:
Tangles and worms of lines creep over the large-format canvases;
gasping breathlessly: is what we see here in front of us
a picture or a drawing?

Painted drawing and the image—
Or actually a picture drawn
with paint on canvas?
A painting because with brush and paint?
That follows naturally!

In Jana's imagination, everything follows naturally:
Rome is located next to Los Angeles and Düsseldorf lies on the Yangtze River!

A wide current meanders yellowish and cloudy, a rivulet of pleasant
stone-gray on the canvas—grows and divides the picture:
Left and right
Top and bottom
Where does a picture begin in the first place? Do these pictures actually
have a defined end?
And where exactly is the top?
Does the image space limit the picture, or does the format of the canvas
frame the image space?

There are no limits in Jana Schröder's art; the extent of her power of
imagination is infinite; Supergirl wins!

The painted drawing is a drawn painting; the picture filled with intermeshed
cryptographic signs, and its network of nerve cells an autonomous image
space 2.0 interwoven with color signals.

Worms entwine the paint-fingered brush, and another picture battles for
its place in the studio and becomes emancipated in the picture labyrinth of
the neon bunker.

Match-ball: Jana Schröder

***Kinkrustation C2***, 2017
Öl auf Leinwand / Oil on canvas
200 × 155 cm / 78.7 × 61 in.

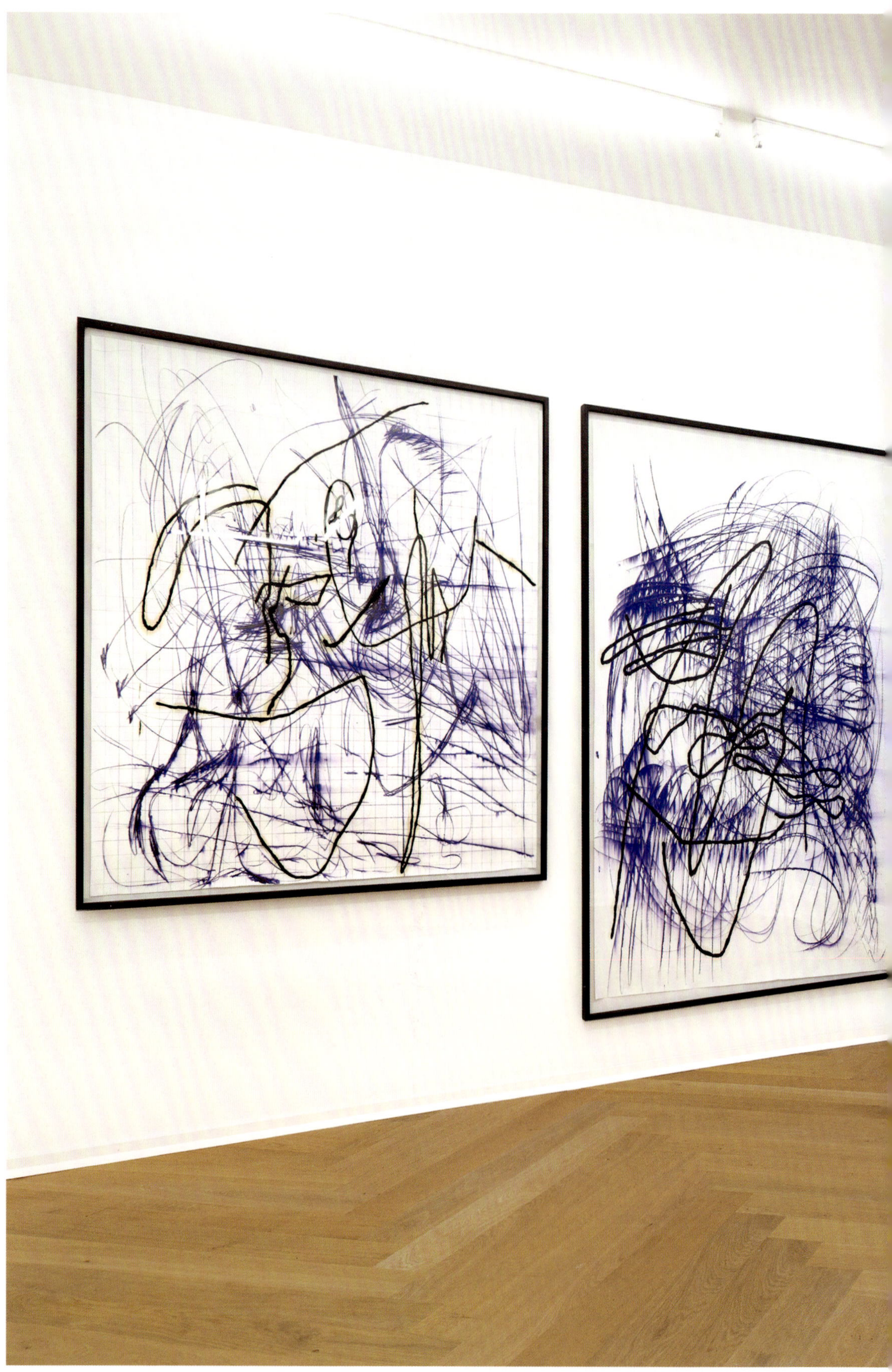

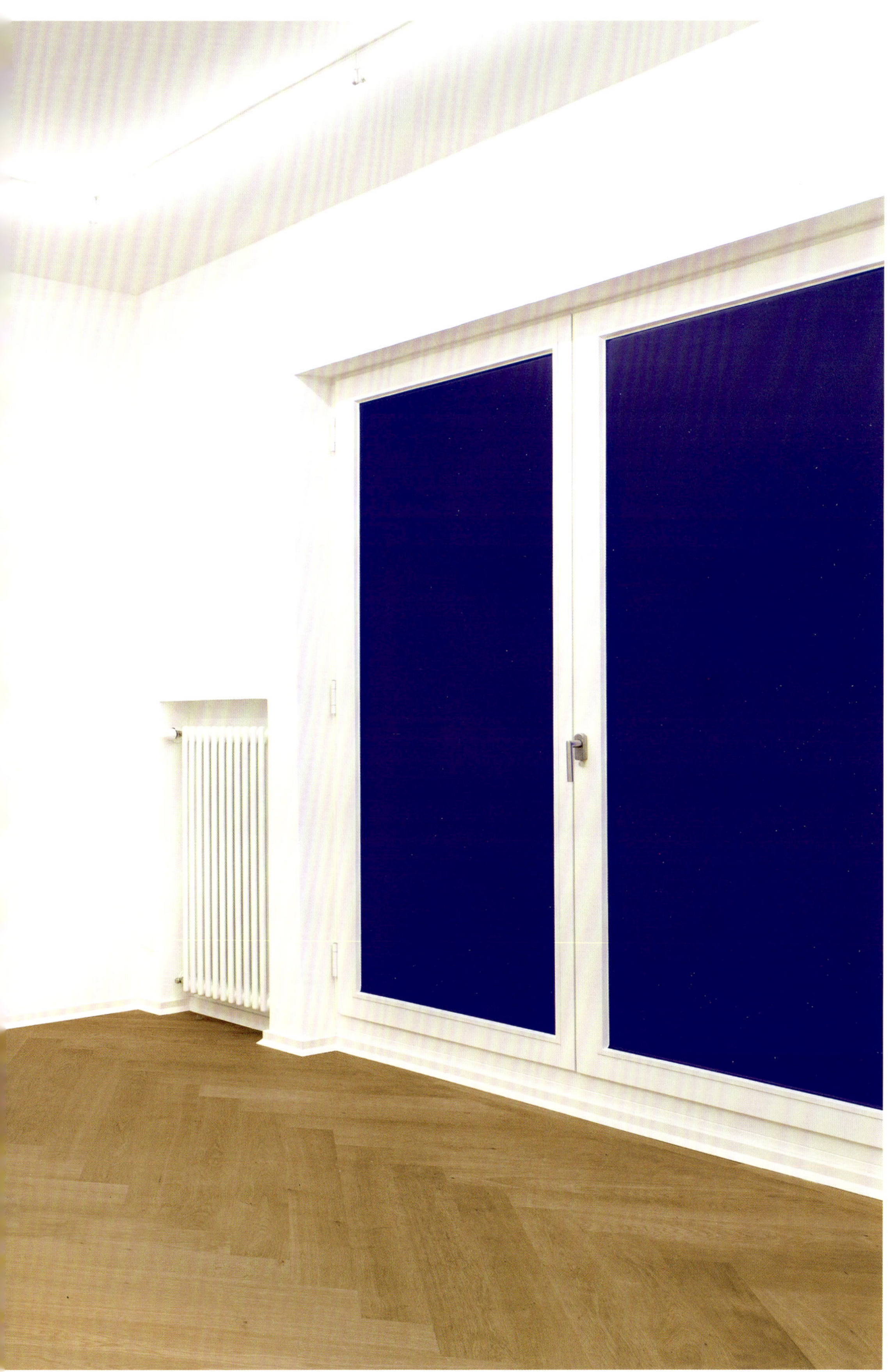

*Spontacts PN1*, 2017
Kopierstift und Öl auf Papier / Copying pencil and oil on paper
200 × 150 cm / 78.7 × 59 in.

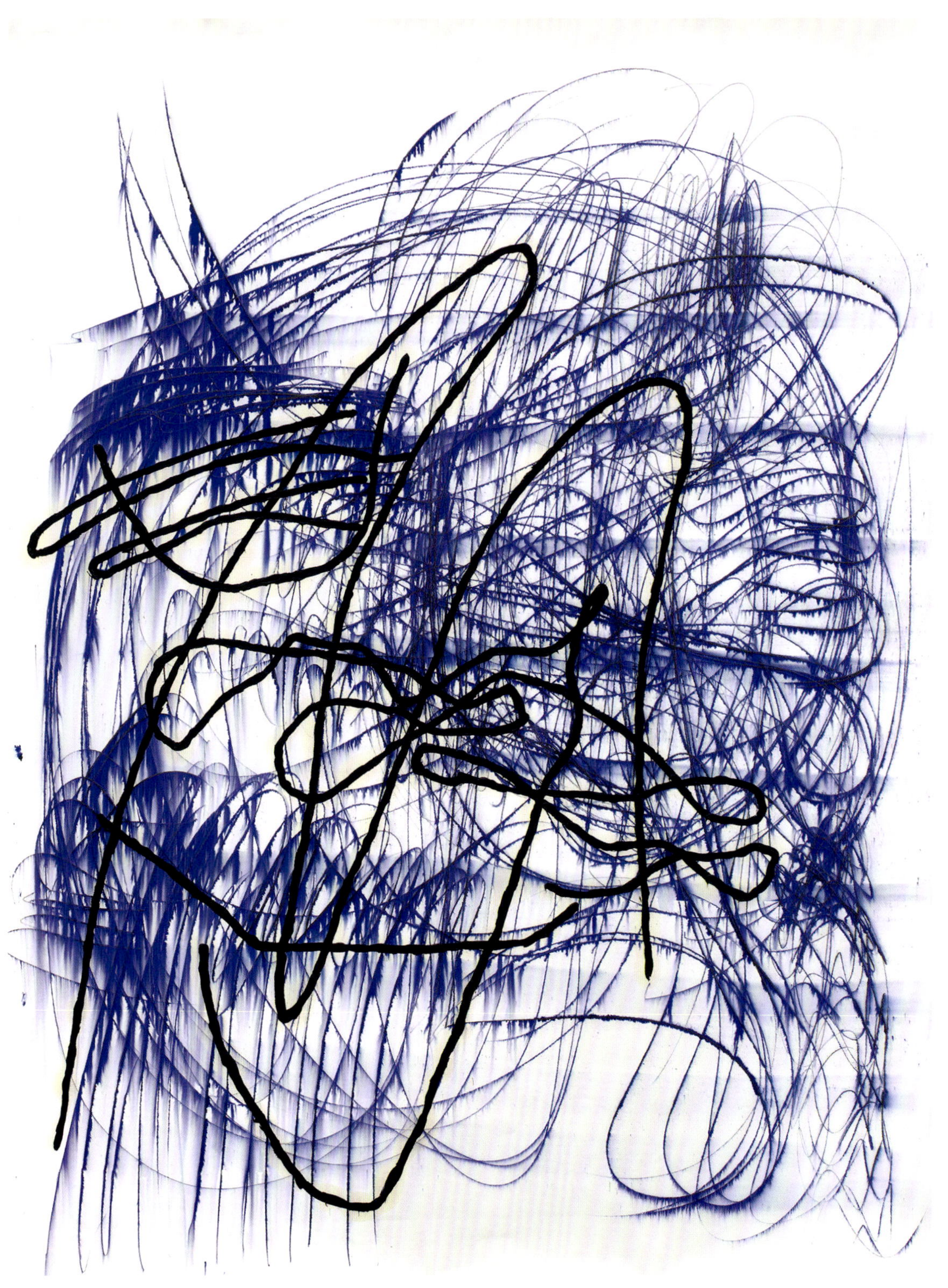

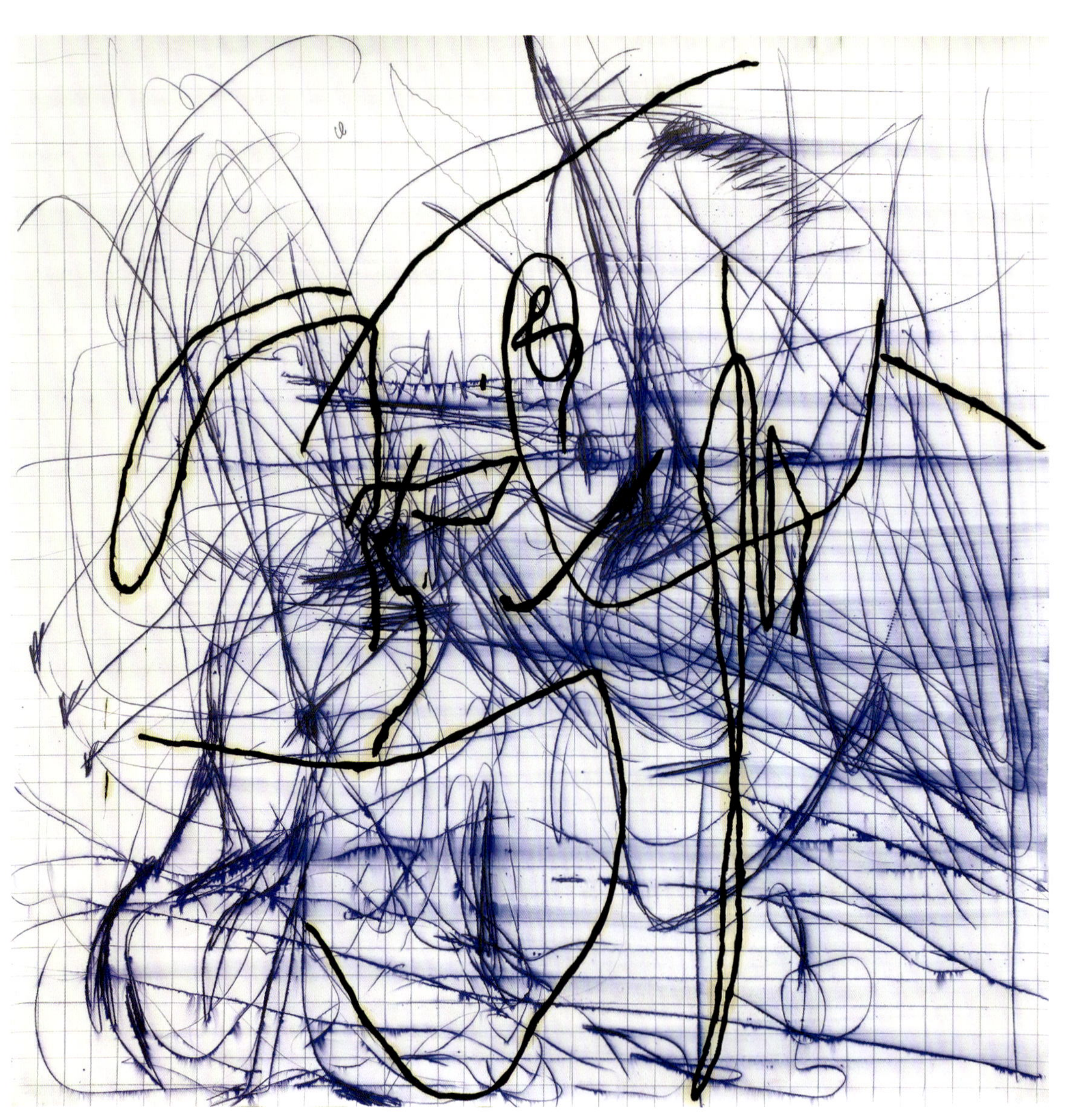

*Spontacts PQN1*, 2017
Kopierstift und Öl auf Papier / Copying pencil and oil on paper
151 × 151 cm / 59.4 × 59.4 in.

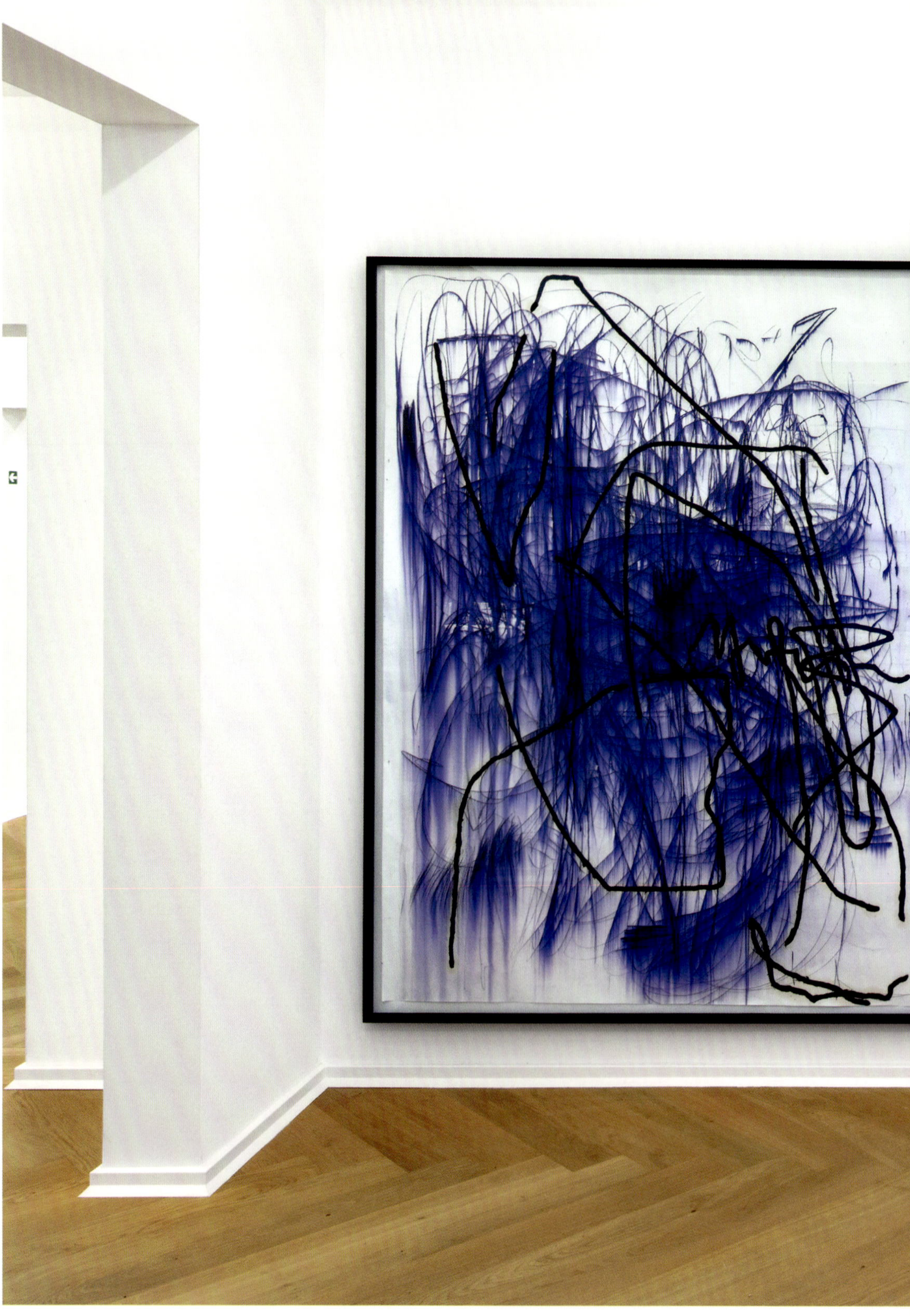

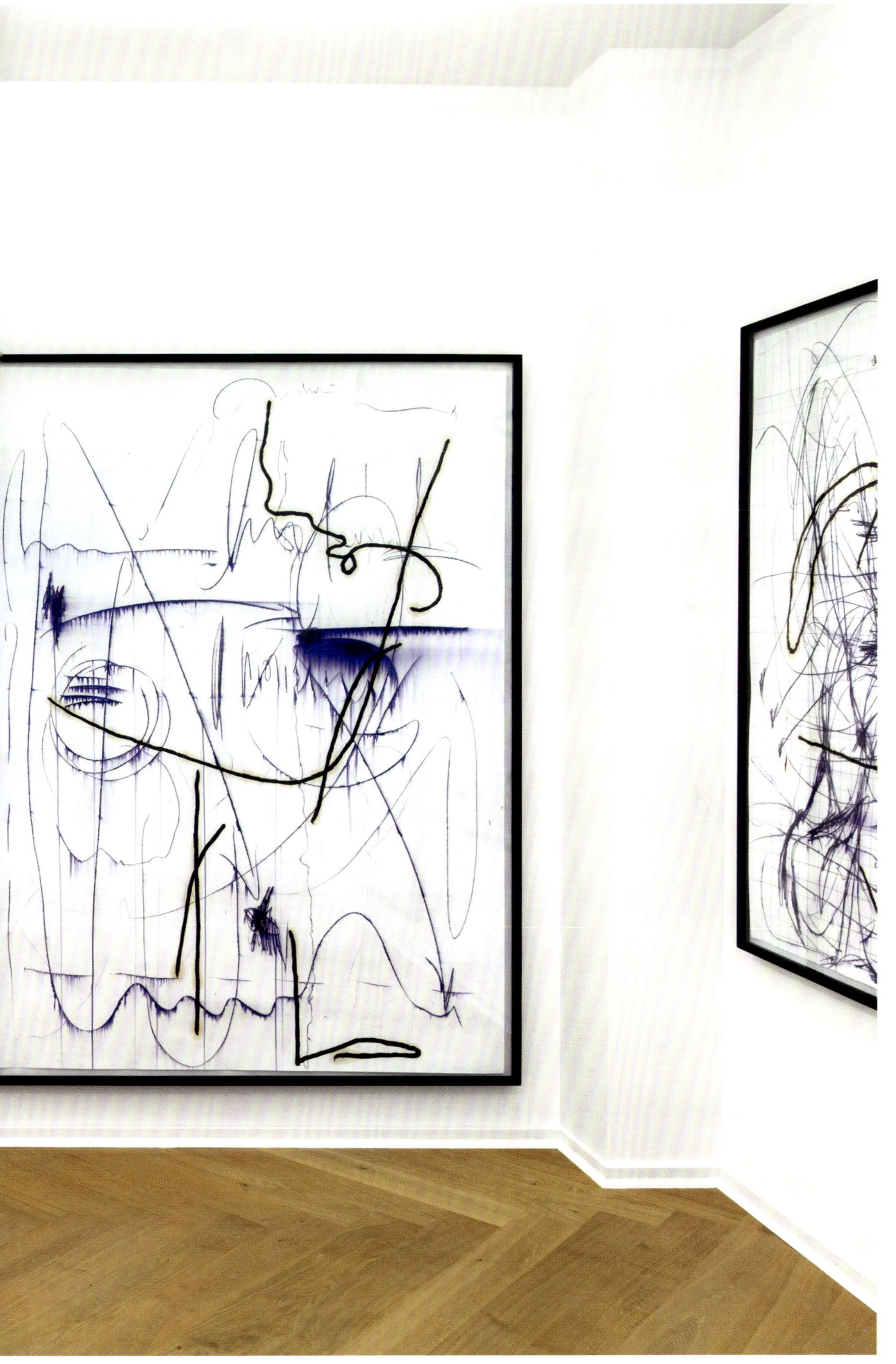

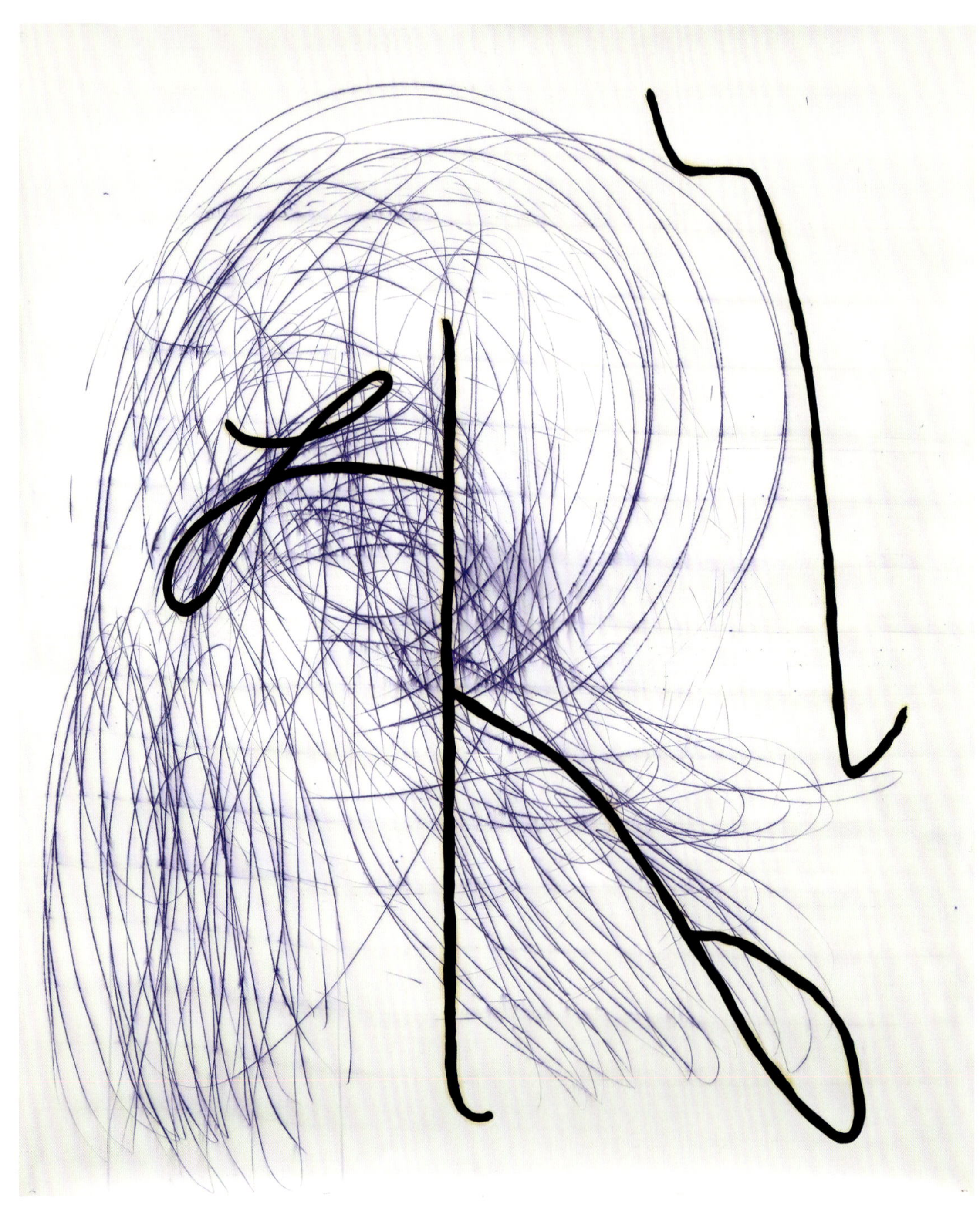

*Spontacts DP 7*, 2015
Kopierstift und Öl auf Papier / Copying pencil and oil on paper
180 × 150 cm / 70.9 × 59 in.

# Reset, Layer-Sehnsucht, Gelato

## *Jana Schröder im Gespräch mit Christian Malycha*

Der Titel Deiner Ausstellung lautet »The Early Years«. Ist der »Jugendbonus« jetzt etwa weg?

**Unbedingt! Der ist schon mit 28 aufgebraucht.**

Wenn wir vor Deinen Bildern stehen, was sehen wir? What's the story?

**Story gibt's nicht.**

Form und Inhalt sind in Deinen Bildern also dasselbe?

**An jeder Serie hab' ich meine persönlichen Bild-Fragestellungen abgearbeitet: Was macht die vertraute Bewegung der Handschrift? Geht's da größtenteils um die Geschwindigkeit? Was passiert, wenn es unleserlich wird? Wie kann man mit der Ästhetik vom Diagrammen umgehen? Was passiert, wenn ich nur zwei Ebenen habe, die zusammenkommen? Was passiert, wenn plötzlich weitere Ebenen hinzukommen, und mir neue Möglichkeiten einfallen, bestimmte Sachen wieder auszulöschen? Was ist los, wenn so viele Farbgeflechte auf die Leinwand kommen, dass es visuell schwer wird, das Ganze in einzelne Elemente zu zerlegen? Schafft es die letzte Ebene, das ganze ›Geschmiere‹ zusammenzuziehen? Ok, so etwa.**

Würde man gar nicht vermuten, dass Deine Bilder so streng gebaut und konzipiert sind.

**Na, das hoffe ich doch, dass einem das nicht sofort unangenehm auffällt!**

Was passiert denn mit der Handschrift, wenn sie unleserlich wird? Was fasziniert Dich an Diagrammen? Stellst Du lieber Regeln auf oder brichst sie?

**Die Handschrift war nur ein Tool, das ich benutzt habe. Die Bewegung der Hand hab' ich ja lang genug trainiert, so dass ich sie am unmittelbarsten einsetzen konnte, eher beiläufig und natürlich. Das ist der Kontrast, den ich zu der sehr bewussten Linie der Ölfarbe haben wollte.**
**Die Ästhetik des Gekritzels ist dazu einfach schön. Ähnlich verhält es sich mit Diagrammen, bei denen dann noch mehr Gekrakel, Gewusel und Pfeile hinzukommen, die irgendwelche Bezüge herstellen. Diagramme habe ich noch nie verstanden, immer nur Schmerzen im Kopf, aber die sehen halt irrsinnig gut aus. Abgesehen davon bilden sie bei den »Spontacts« durch die hinzugefügte Gitterstruktur eine zusätzliche dritte Ebene, die dazu dient, die erste Kopierstiftebene deutlicher abzuschließen.**
**Und Regeln stelle ich genauso gerne auf, wie ich sie anschließend wieder breche. Daraus wird dann eben die neu angepasste Regel.**

Jetzt zeigst Du Werke aus den vergangenen 10 Jahren und es gibt chronologische Kapitel. Was für Bilder hast Du ausgesucht?

**Mit einem Bild aus der »Kinkrustations«-Serie fängt es an. Die »Spontacts« hängen in einem eigenen Raum mit blaugetönter Fensterscheibe. Auch einige der Arbeiten, die in der Ausstellung bei Dir im Kunstverein Reutlingen hingen. Damals Unterkante, jetzt Oberkante. Man muss ja flexibel bleiben ... Es gibt drei »Kadlites« mit sehr verschiedenen Ansätzen, aber auch noch zwei frühe, eher untypisch auf Holzplatten, die sich ziemlich von den späteren unterscheiden.**

Retrospektiv ist die Ausstellung aber nur zum Teil. Es gibt auch ganz neue Gemälde und Papierarbeiten, die noch nie gezeigt wurden.

**Ja, dazwischen hängen einige kleine Papierarbeiten. So kleine hab' ich ewig nicht gemacht. Die sind entstanden, als die »Kadlites« ausgepinselt waren, und führen zu den ganz neuen »Neurosox«. Zu denen gehört das letzte Bild im Karminzimmer. Das einzige, das ich für die Ausstellung und speziell für diesen Raum gemalt habe. Fand' ich jetzt ganz gut, die dazu zu hängen, da sie sich alle gegenseitig bedingen und es ja immer weiter geht.**

Vielfalt und Zusammenhang?

**Ja, ist doch super! Ich hab' die ja auch noch nie alle zusammen gesehen.**

Also Selbstüberprüfung und Selbstverunsicherung?

**Ich bin eigentlich eher eine Verfechterin davon, unterschiedliche Serien nicht zu vermischen. In den Räumen der Stiftung funktioniert das aber sehr gut. Selbstüberprüfung ist also schon nicht falsch. Zudem läuft man da immer im Kreis. Das geht sogar mehrfach ... Und ohne Selbstverunsicherung würde gar nichts abgehen, die ist immer eine feine Sache.**

Kannst Du etwas zu den unterschiedlichen Werkgruppen sagen? Du hast erzählt, die ersten »Spontacts« sind als Schriftbilder entstanden. Nur werden die Gesten der Handschrift unmittelbar zu gestischen Figuren, Text wird Textur. Wie kam das?

**Auf den allerersten »Spontacts« gibt es tatsächlich noch ein paar Buchstaben, meist auf dem Kopf oder spiegelverkehrt, manchmal auch mit Schreibfehlern. Weil es aber nie um Schrift im Sinne eines Hinweises ging, waren die sehr schnell nicht mehr lesbar.**

Während die »Spontacts« fast immateriell erscheinen, sind die »Kinkrustations« das krasse Gegenteil dazu: massiv und geschlossen, schwer und pastos verdichtet. Ganz offensichtlich war es Dir ein Bedürfnis, der Offenheit und Leichtigkeit der »Spontacts« etwas entgegenzusetzen.

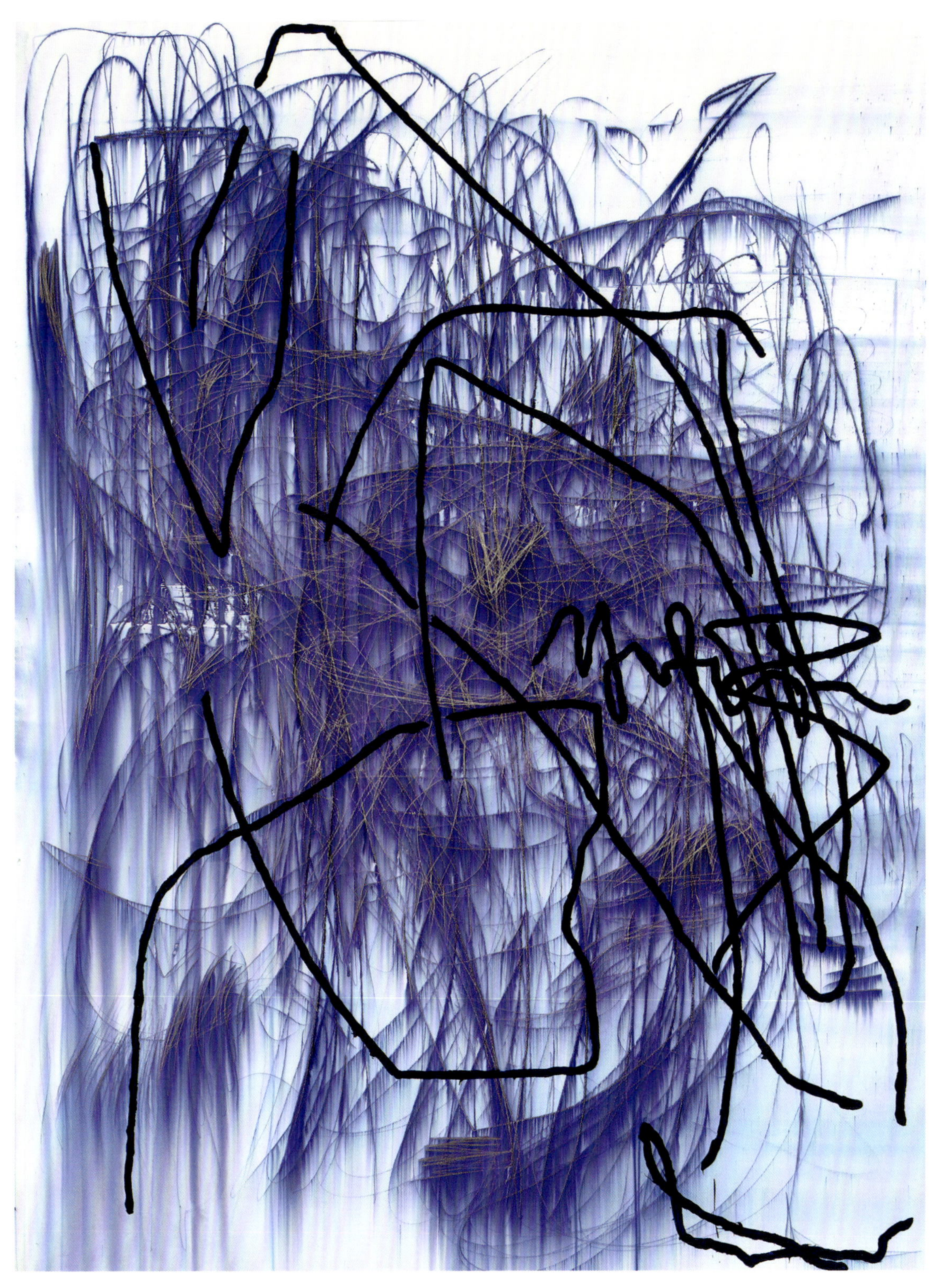

*Spontacts PR5*, 2016
Kopierstift und Öl auf Papier / Copying pencil and oil on paper
200 × 150 cm / 78.8 × 59 in.

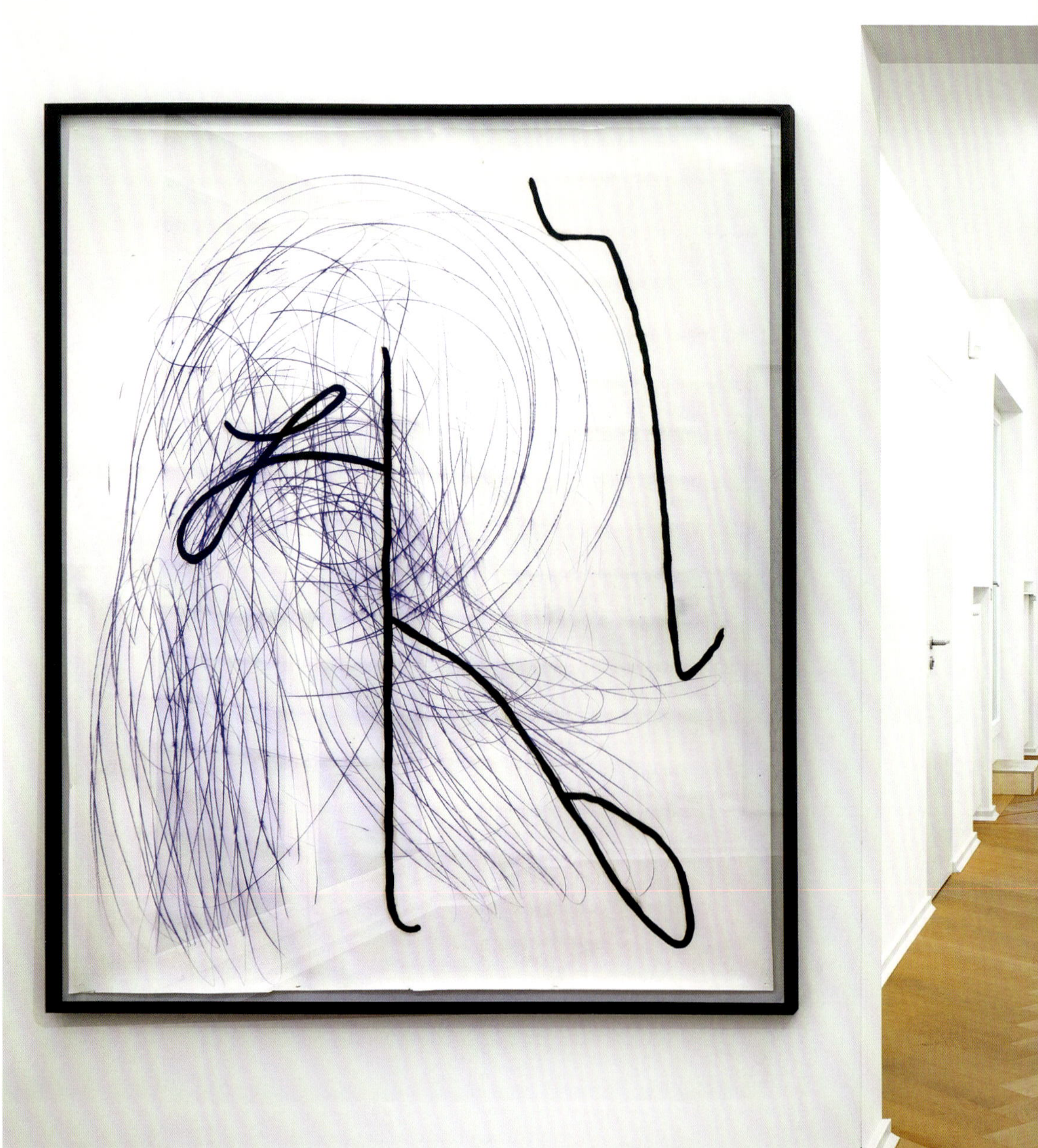

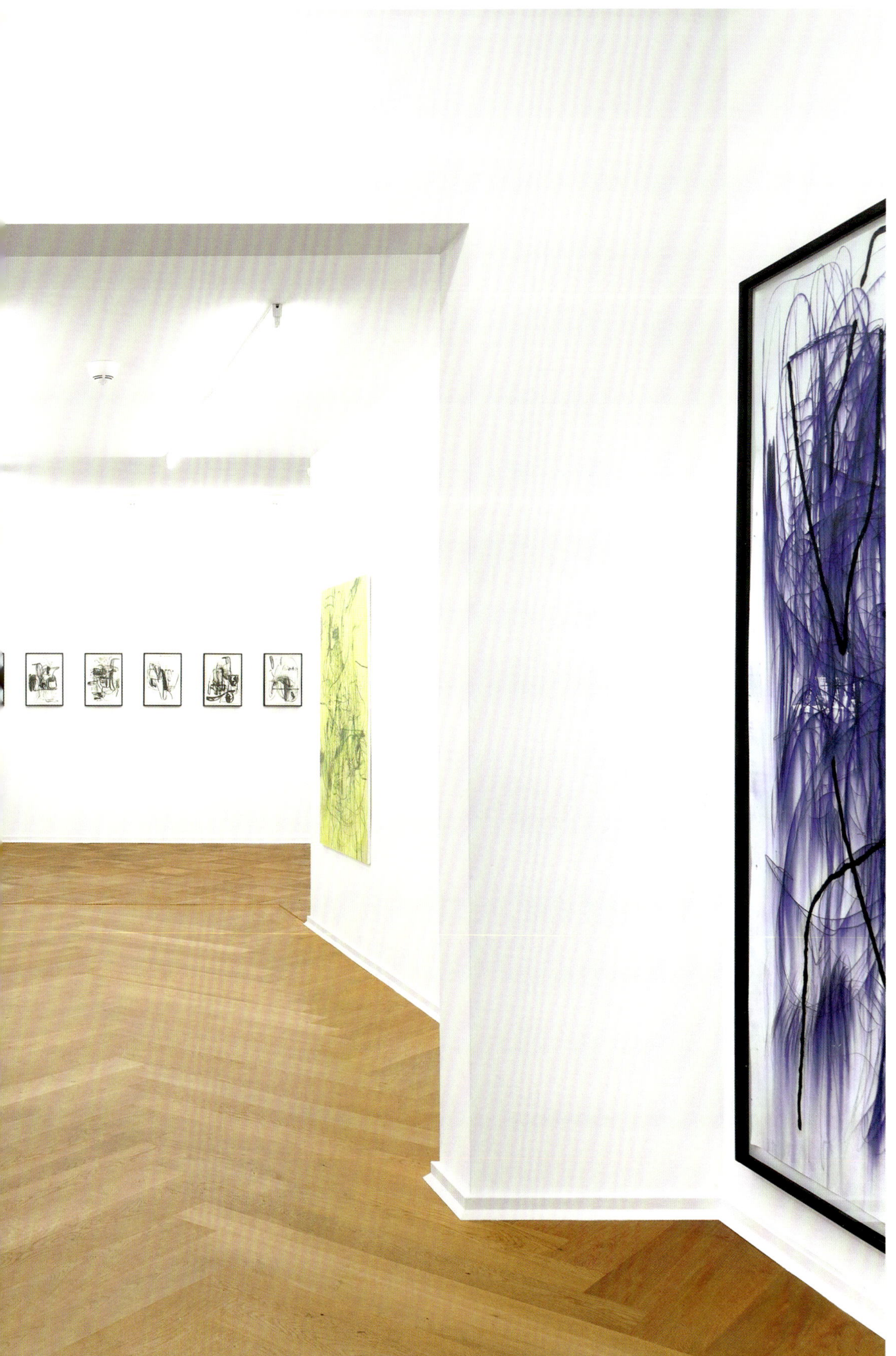

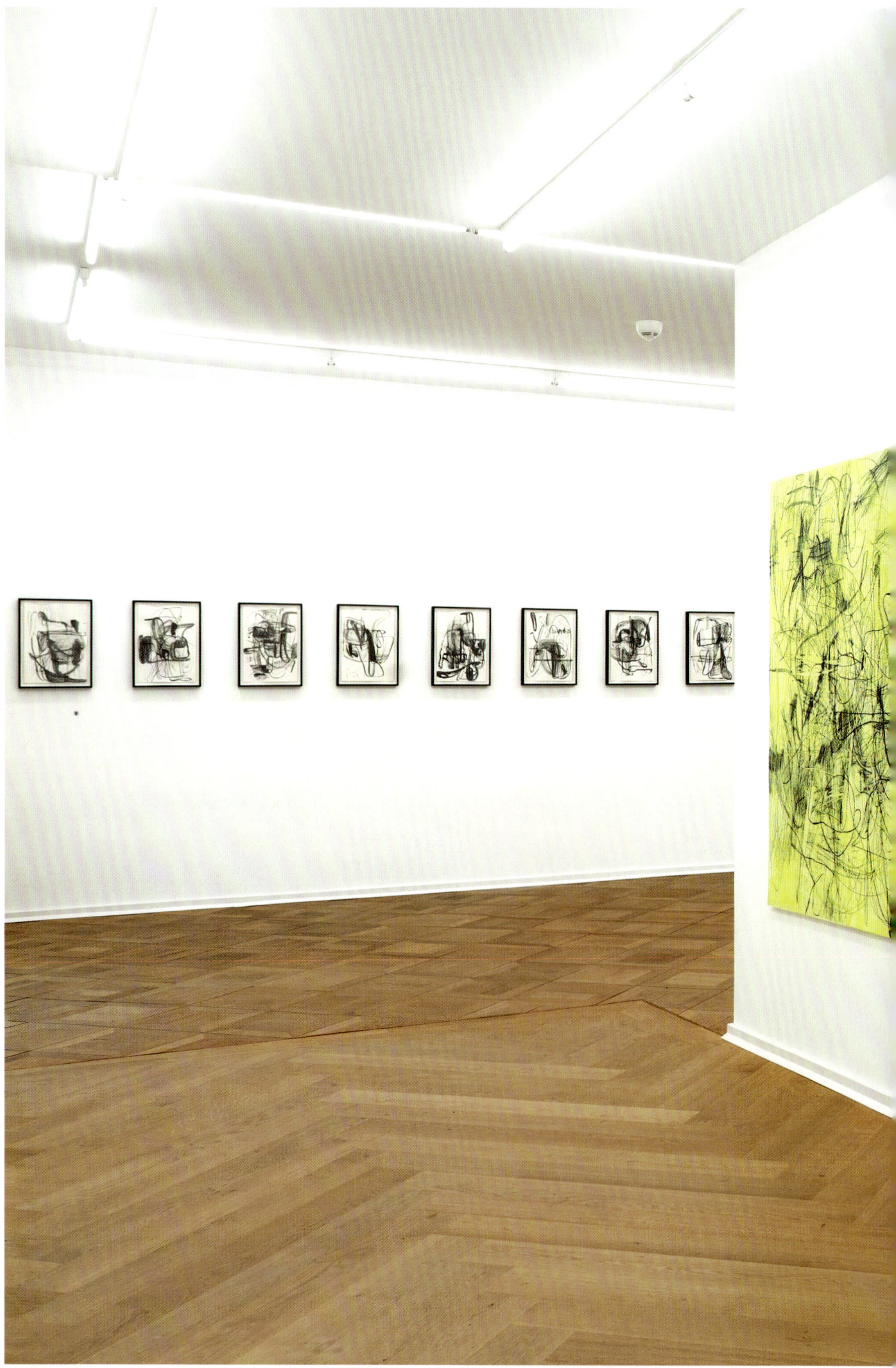

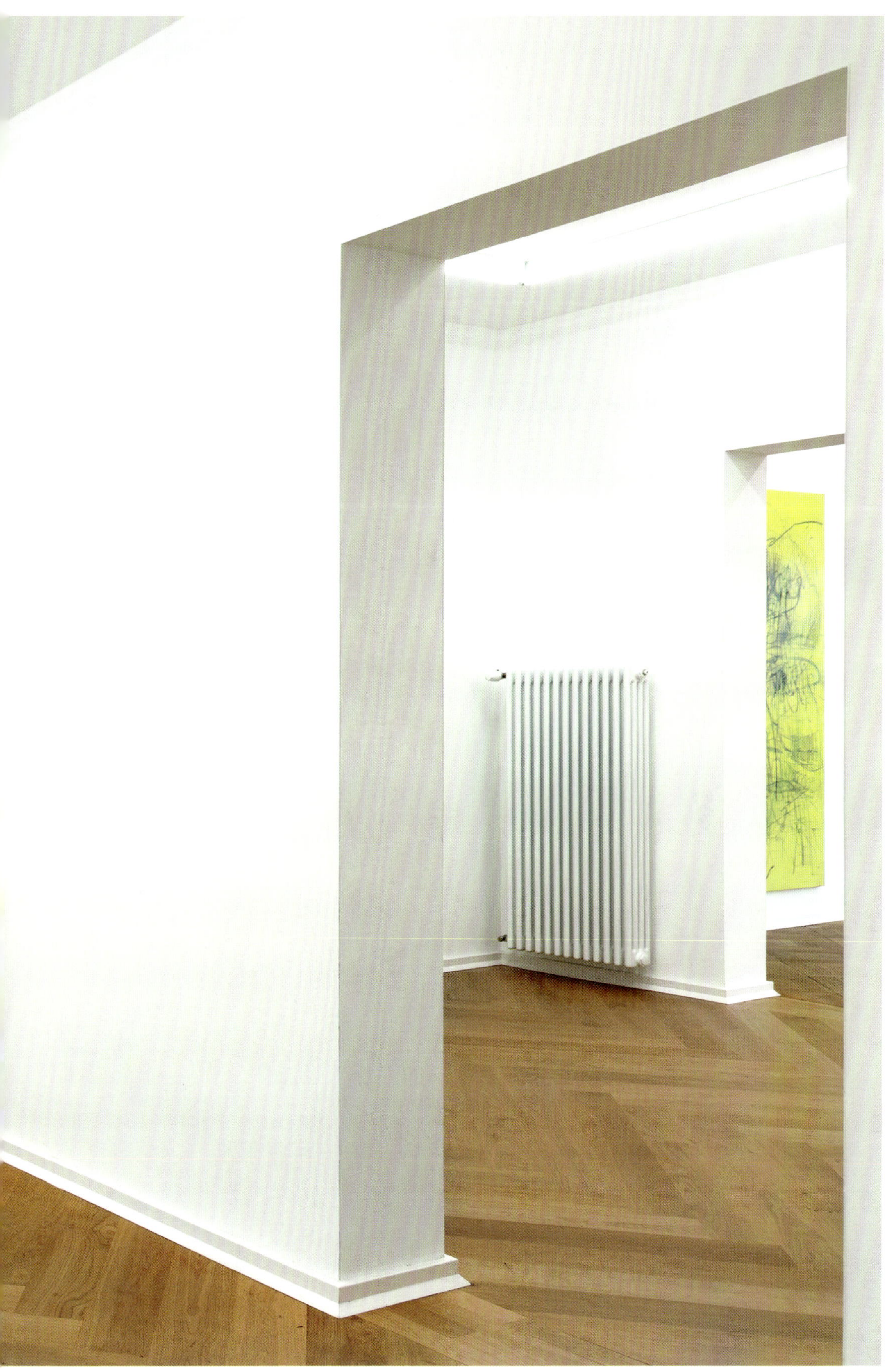

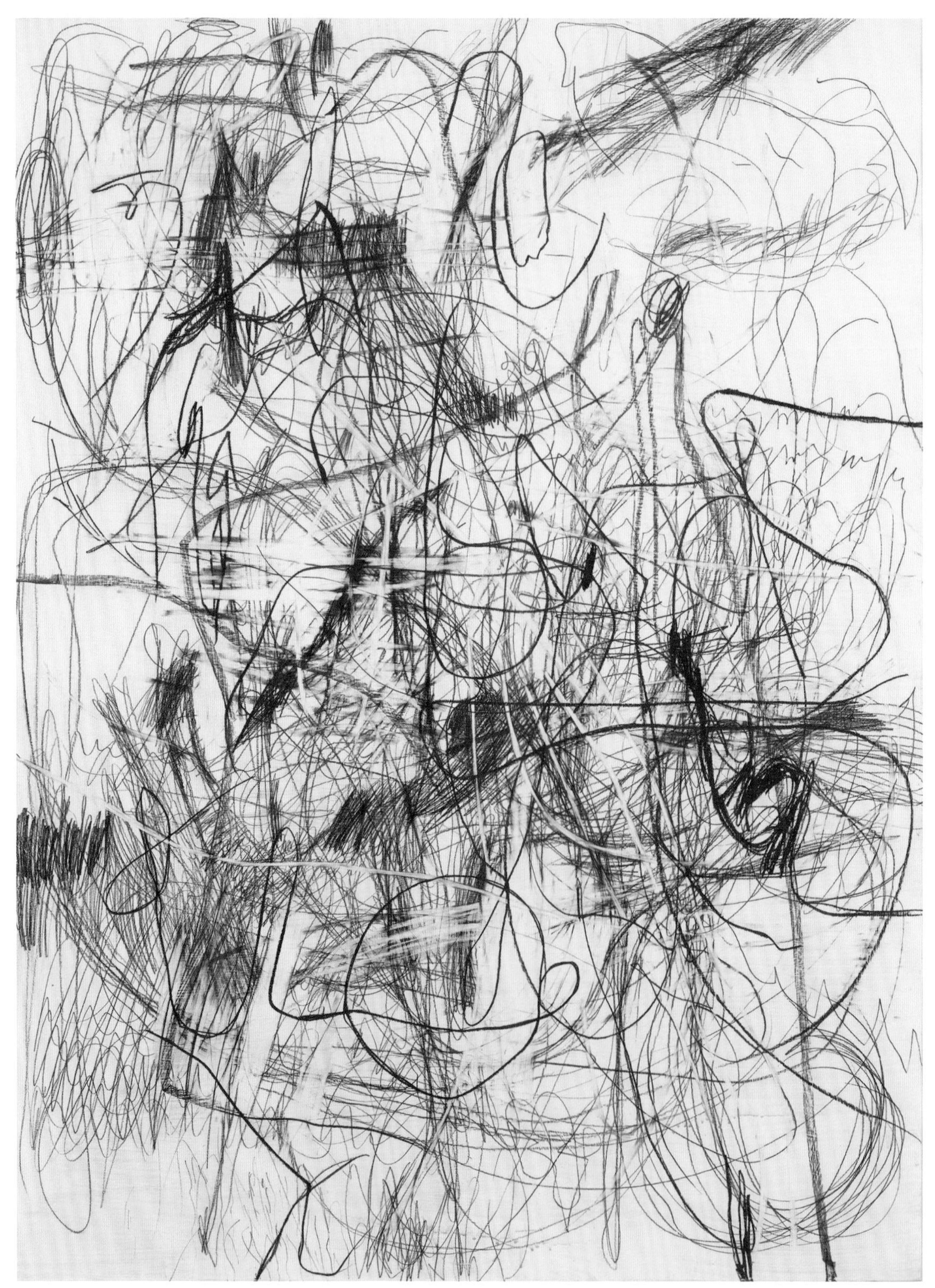

*Kadlites H1*, 2017
Acryl, Grafit und Blei auf Holz / Acrylic, graphite, and lead on wood
140 × 104 cm / 55.1 × 40.9 in.

**Genau, beide Serien sind zeitgleich entstanden und selbst bei den »Kinkrustations« geht es vor allem um die Linie. Nur ist das viel schwieriger zu entschlüsseln als bei den »Spontacts«. Manchmal ist es auch gar nicht mehr nachvollziehbar. Es sind unterschiedliche Geschwindigkeiten: bewusste Beschleunigung, bewusste Verlangsamung.**

Linien, die sich auflösen, und Linien, die sich verdichten?

**So ist es.**

2017 kommen beide ans Ende und die ersten »Kadlites« entstehen.

**Mit den »Kadlites« hatte ich bereits 2011 begonnen, nur damals erstmal zur Seite gestellt. Doch zuletzt war das Blau der »Spontacts« so schön, dass ich endlich bereit war, mit diesem profanen Gelb weiterzumachen.**

Warum Gelb?

**Gelb ist ja eine richtig dämliche Farbe. Allerdings war es die einzige Farbe, bei der die Lasuren, die ich haben wollte, funktionierten. Es schluckt etwas, lässt aber auch noch genug durchkommen.**

Das war der Reiz?

**Die »Spontacts« haben ja fast ausschließlich nur zwei Ebenen: Kopierstift und anschließend Ölfarbe auf dem Kopierstift. Da hatte ich überhaupt keine Möglichkeit, irgendetwas zu korrigieren. Zumindest nicht, indem ich etwas löschte oder visuell ungeschehen machte. Auf dem Weiß sieht man ja alles. Die ›Korrektur‹ bestand vielmehr darin, mit dem am Ende aufgetragenen, langsamen Ölstrich den Fehlern auf der Kopierstiftebene etwas entgegenzusetzen. Oder sie erst richtig zu betonen. Das war meine Aufgabenstellung.**
**Eine minimale Ausnahme sind, wie schon gesagt, die »Ultra-Diagrams« mit ihren 3 Ebenen.**
**Nach einer Weile überkam mich dann aber eine regelrechte Layer-Sehnsucht. Sieht man ja, die »Kadlites« können bis zu 17 Ebenen haben. Und ich hab's mir sogar wieder gegönnt, etwas ›radieren‹ zu können. Das Beste dabei ist, dass die radierten Stellen zu etwas ganz Eigenem werden.**

Das führt 2019 zu den »Neurosox«. Die Farbe schwindet jedoch wieder. Die Bilder sind schwarzweiß.

**Das war, glaube ich, ein Reset.**

Und sie werden plötzlich malerisch.

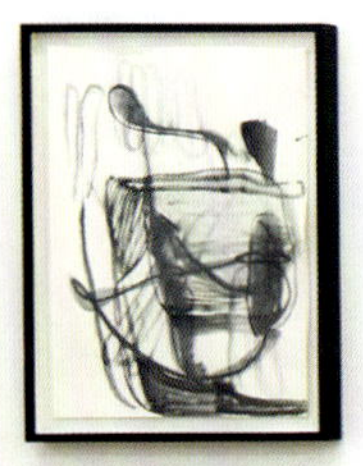
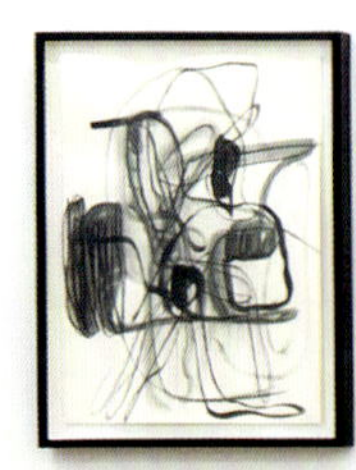
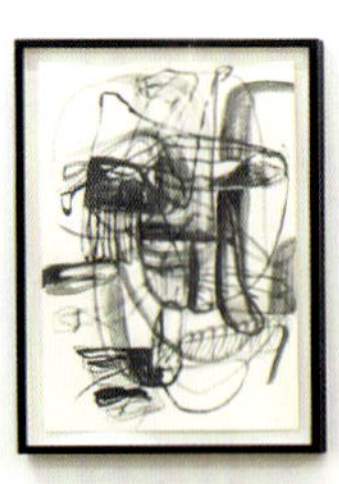
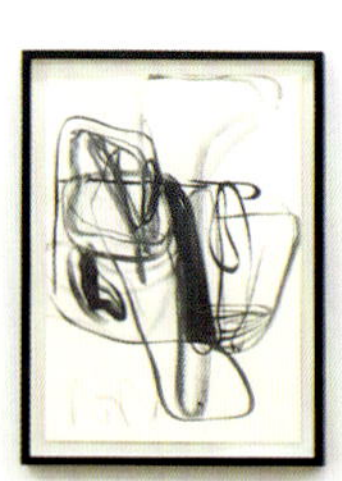
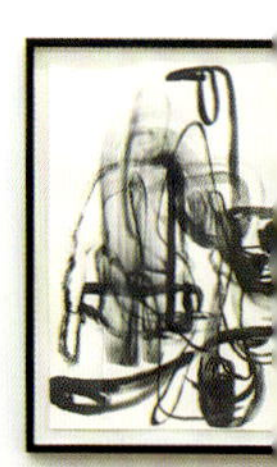

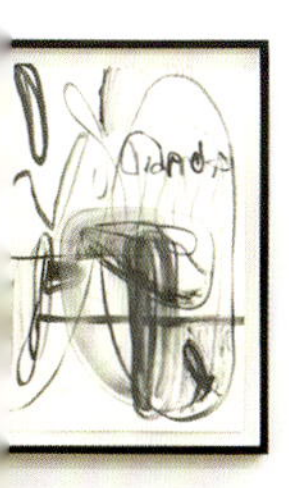
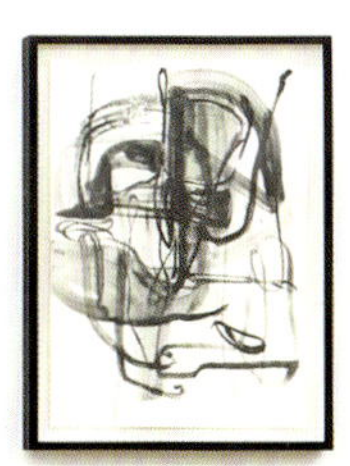
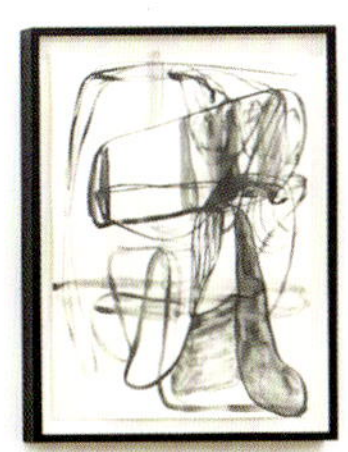
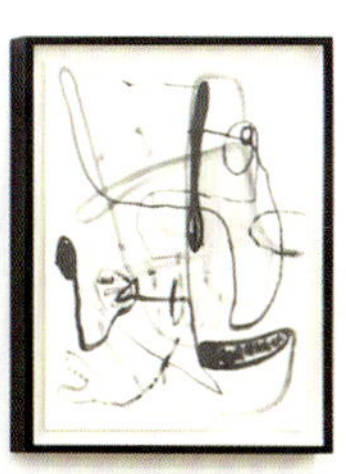
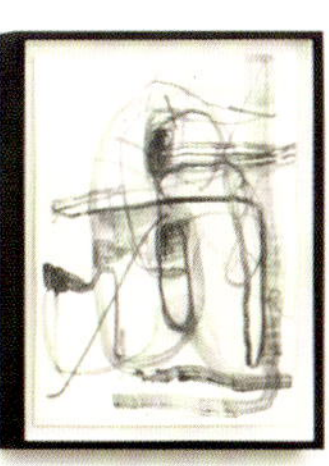

**Nachdem ich jetzt so lange rumgekritzelt hab', hatte ich schlichtweg richtig Bock auf Malerei. Das fing schon bei den späteren »Kadlites« an. Die Lasuren haben viel Fläche verschluckt, aber die korrigierten Stellen, die Stellen, an denen die Linien ausgelöscht worden sind, waren immer Fläche. Und ab einer gewissen Breite der Linie kann man sich sowieso überlegen, ob das nicht eher Malerei ist.**

Erstaunlich ist das Grau, das so gewieft nuanciert ist, dass es ständig die Ebenen gegeneinander verschiebt und die Balance im Bild immer neu verhandelt.

**Das ist das Bleipulver. Die meisten »Neurosox« sind nur mit weißer Farbe und Bleipulver gemacht. Das Bleipulver ist unkaputtbar. Mischt sich überall ein. Das gefällt mir.**

Mit den »Specshifts« dann eine noch deutlichere Verschiebung der Eigenschaften. Wie grundsätzlich ist dieser Wandel?

**Zwischen »Neurosox« und »Specshifts« würde ich gar keinen Wandel sehen wollen. An beiden arbeite ich ja noch.**

Dieselbe Sache? Einmal Schwarzweiß, einmal in Farbe?

**Grob gesagt schon. Farbkontraste machen was anderes als das Helldunkel. Und durch die Farbe nehme ich noch mehr Malerei mit rein.**

Bislang gab es gestische Zeichen auf oder vor einem einfarbigen Grund. Die »Specshifts« sind nicht chromatisch angelegt, sondern bauen auf Kontrasten auf. Die Farbbeziehungen sind um ein Vielfaches komplexer. Das erinnert mich an Bilder von Dir aus dem Studium …

**Ja, mich auch … Im Anschluss an die »Spontacts« hab' ich ja bereits auf etwas zurückgegriffen, das ich zuvor gemacht habe, und an die Gelben angeknüpft. Das war möglich, weil die »Kadlites« damals noch nicht zu Ende gedacht waren. Danach war das ähnlich. Um mir etwas Neues zu erarbeiten, hab' ich zunächst ganz viel zugelassen. Dabei geht auch mal was schief. Die vorherigen Arbeiten funktionierten, methodisch und stringent, nur dann sind plötzlich wieder alle Türen offen und alle Möglichkeiten zurück. Da muss man erstmal aussortieren.**

Die grafischen Texturen werden in den »Neurosox« und »Specshifts« zu einem verschlungenen Gewebe mit enormer Weite und Tiefe.

**Die Ebenen verwurschteln sich jetzt ja auch. Weite und Tiefe haben mich früher überhaupt nicht interessiert, eher gestört. Ich hab' noch nicht mal über den Rand gepinselt und die gesamte Fläche gleichbehandelt. Jetzt muss ich wohl bald wieder etwas mehr aufpassen.**

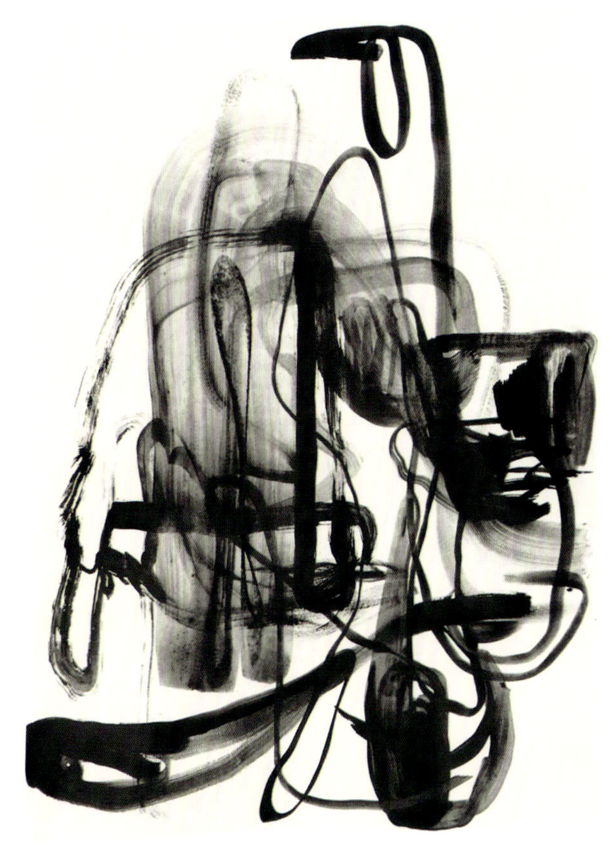

*DK 15*, 2020
Tusche auf Papier / Ink on paper
42 × 29 cm / 16.5 × 11.4 in.

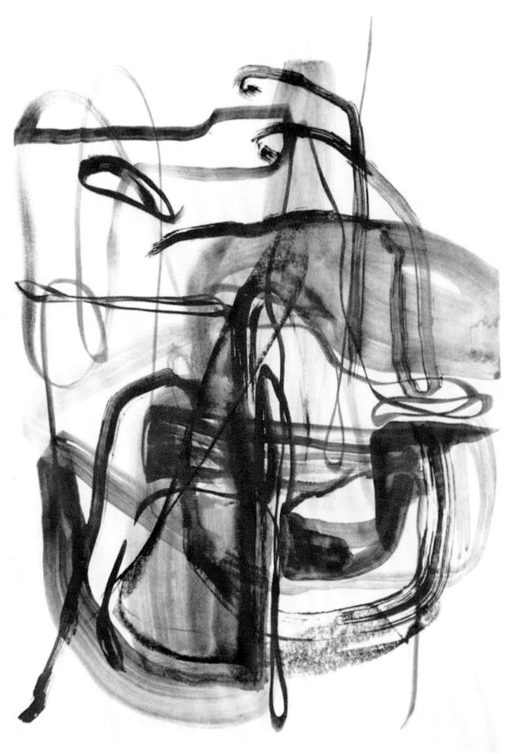

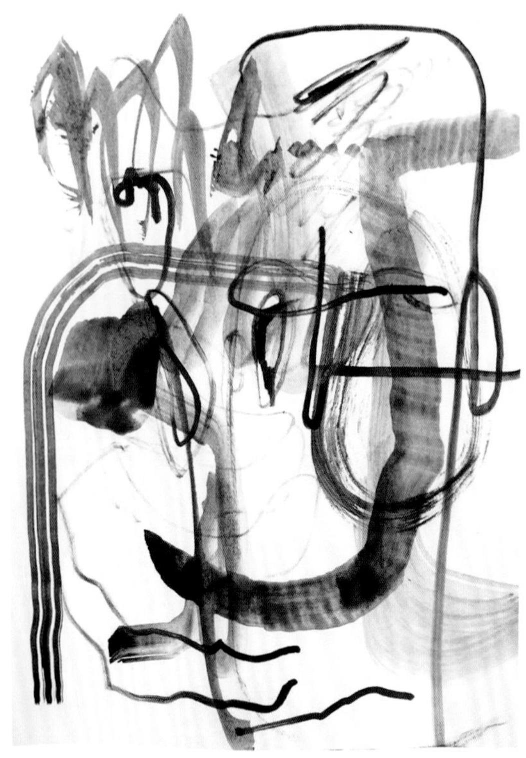

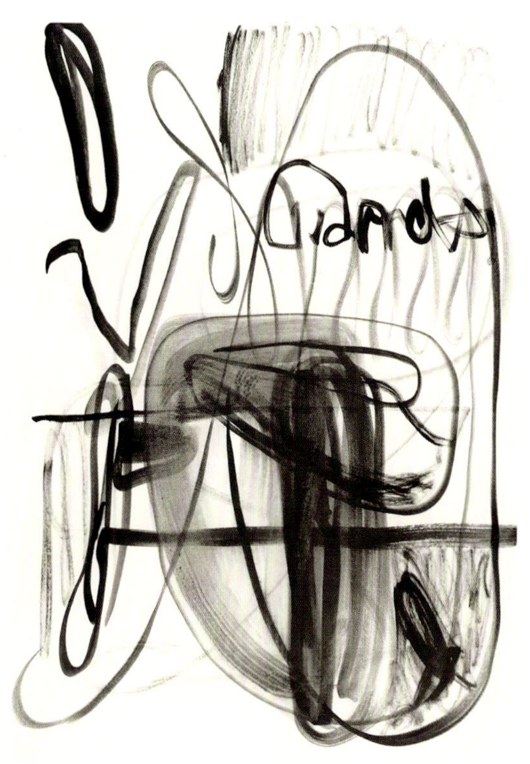

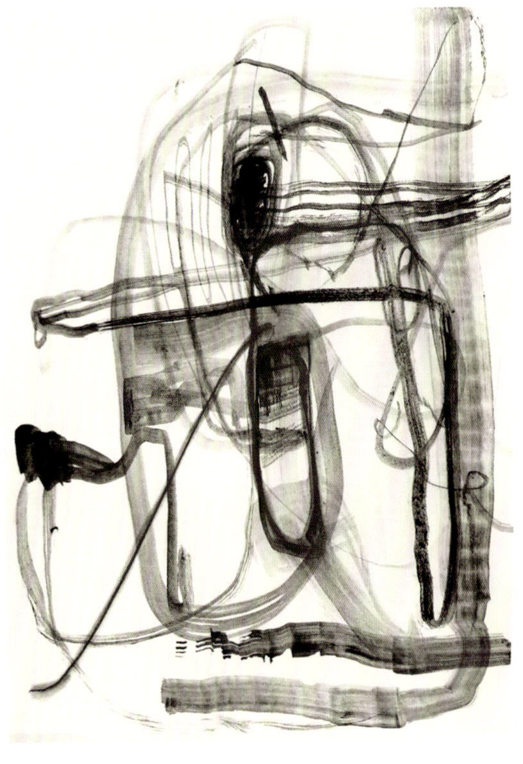

*DK 24*, *DK 25*, *DK 27*, *DK 28*, 2020
Tusche auf Papier / Ink on paper
je / each 42 × 29 cm / 16.5 × 11.4 in.

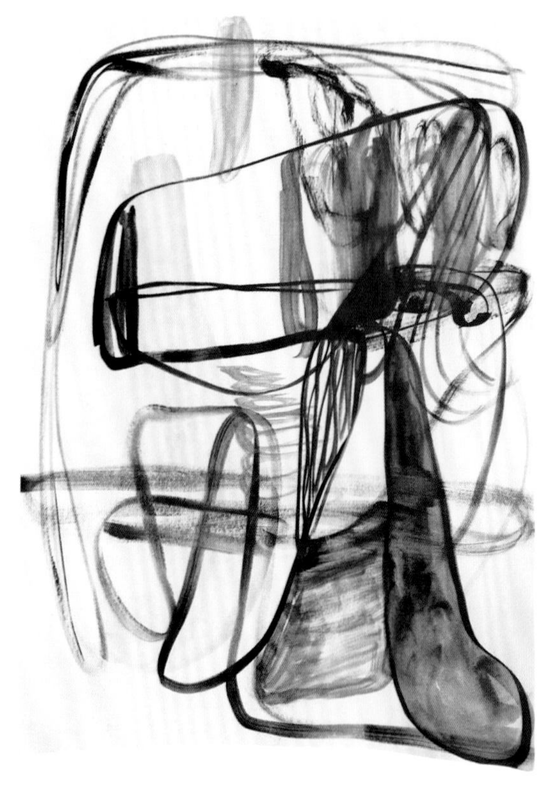

*DK 43*, 2020
Tusche auf Papier / Ink on paper
42 × 29 cm / 16.5 × 11.4 in.

**Denn, wenn ich jetzt wieder ein paar mehr Farben hinzunehme, ist die Frage natürlich, was da noch von den alten Regeln und Routinen bleibt. Manches, das vorher voll gut ging, geht gar nicht mehr. Manches geht aber auch wieder und zwar so richtig.**

Die neuen Bilder sind ziemlich umwerfend. Reißen die Dich selbst auch mit?

**Ich muss es leider zugeben, wie ein Wildbach!**

Wollte man die letzten zehn Jahre zusammenfassen: Linie wird flächig. Helldunkel wird kontrastfarbig. Grafisches wird malerisch. Bildfelder werden Bildräume. Korrekt?

**Schon.**

Woran erkennst Du, dass ein Bild abgeschlossen ist?

**Ich arbeite immer an mehreren Bildern gleichzeitig und wenn eins ein paar Tage im Atelier steht und ich nichts mehr finde, das anders sein sollte, dann ist es fertig.**

Mir scheint es trotzdem manchmal, als wären Deine Bilder immer mitten in einer unabgeschlossenen Bewegung, immer zwischen Kommen und Gehen, Entstehen und Vergehen.

**Kommt mir auch so vor. Ich bin sehr fahrig und es wird auch immer schlimmer.**

Du arbeitest in Serien, schon immer und konsequent. Sogar die Formate bleiben über die Jahre ziemlich konstant. Trotzdem ist jedes Bild unverwechselbar und individuell.

**Die Formate bleiben gleich, weil ich faul bin. 240 × 200 cm ist groß genug und trotzdem noch einfach zu bewegen. Kleiner ist meistens schwieriger und größer geht immer gut. Hinzukommt, dass ich so ein stumpfer Typ bin und es immer besser ertragen kann, wenn mehrere Bilder desselben Formats nebeneinander hängen. Dann werden bei einer Serie von Bild zu Bild auch die Unterschiede sichtbarer, klar. Ich hab' bei jedem Bild etwas anderes rausgefunden und die Ausreißer bringen da häufig am meisten.**

Wie ›expressiv‹, wie ›konzeptuell‹ sind Deine Bilder?

**Ich glaube, das hält sich die Waage. Wenn eine expressive Geste stehen bleibt, dann ist das ja automatisch Teil der Haltung. Meist beginne ich expressiv ... Wobei ich das Wort eigentlich lieber vermeiden würde und ersetzen durch: Meist geht's roh los ... und alle folgenden Entscheidungen grenzen dann ein und werden immer bewusster.**

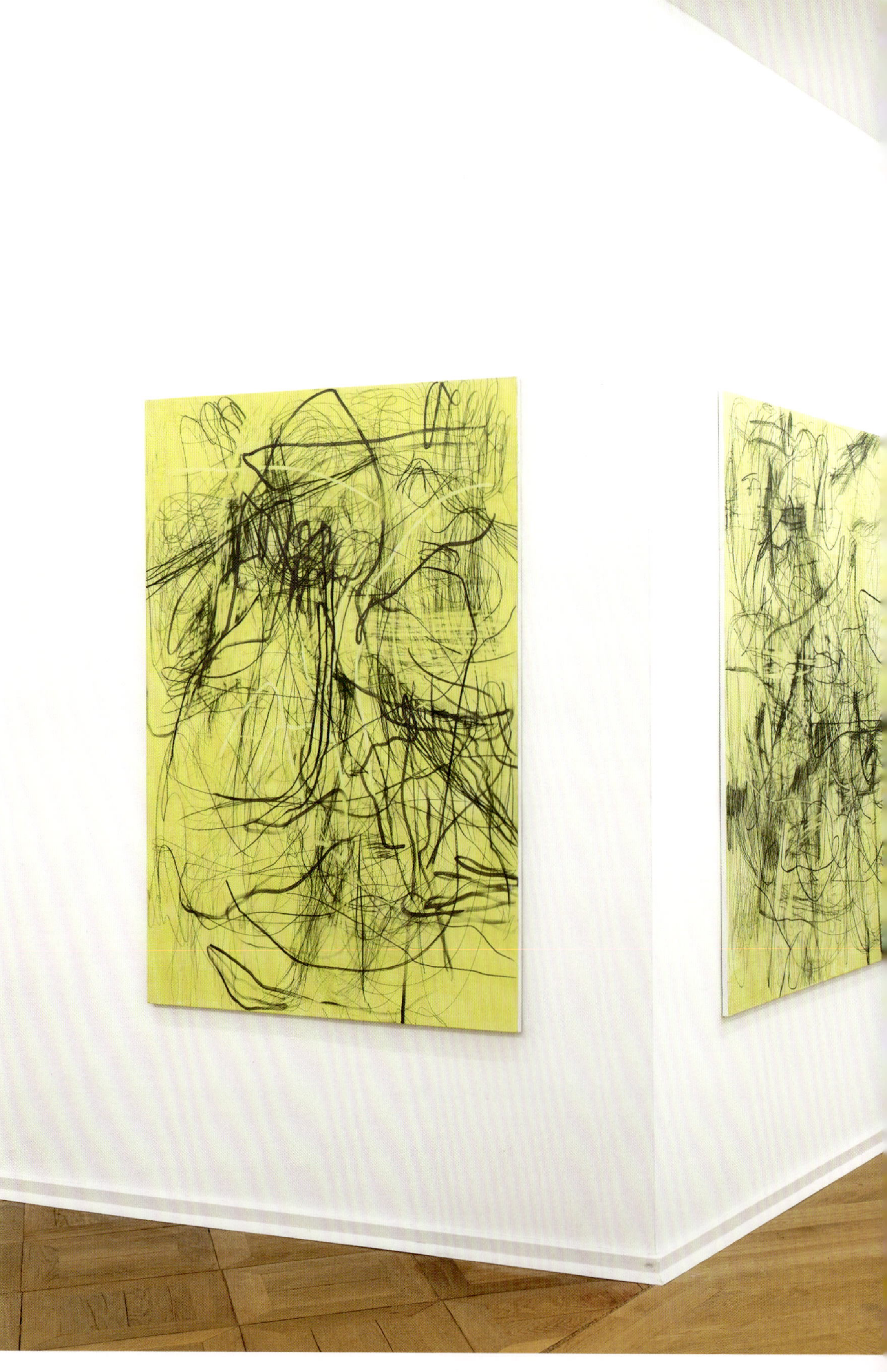

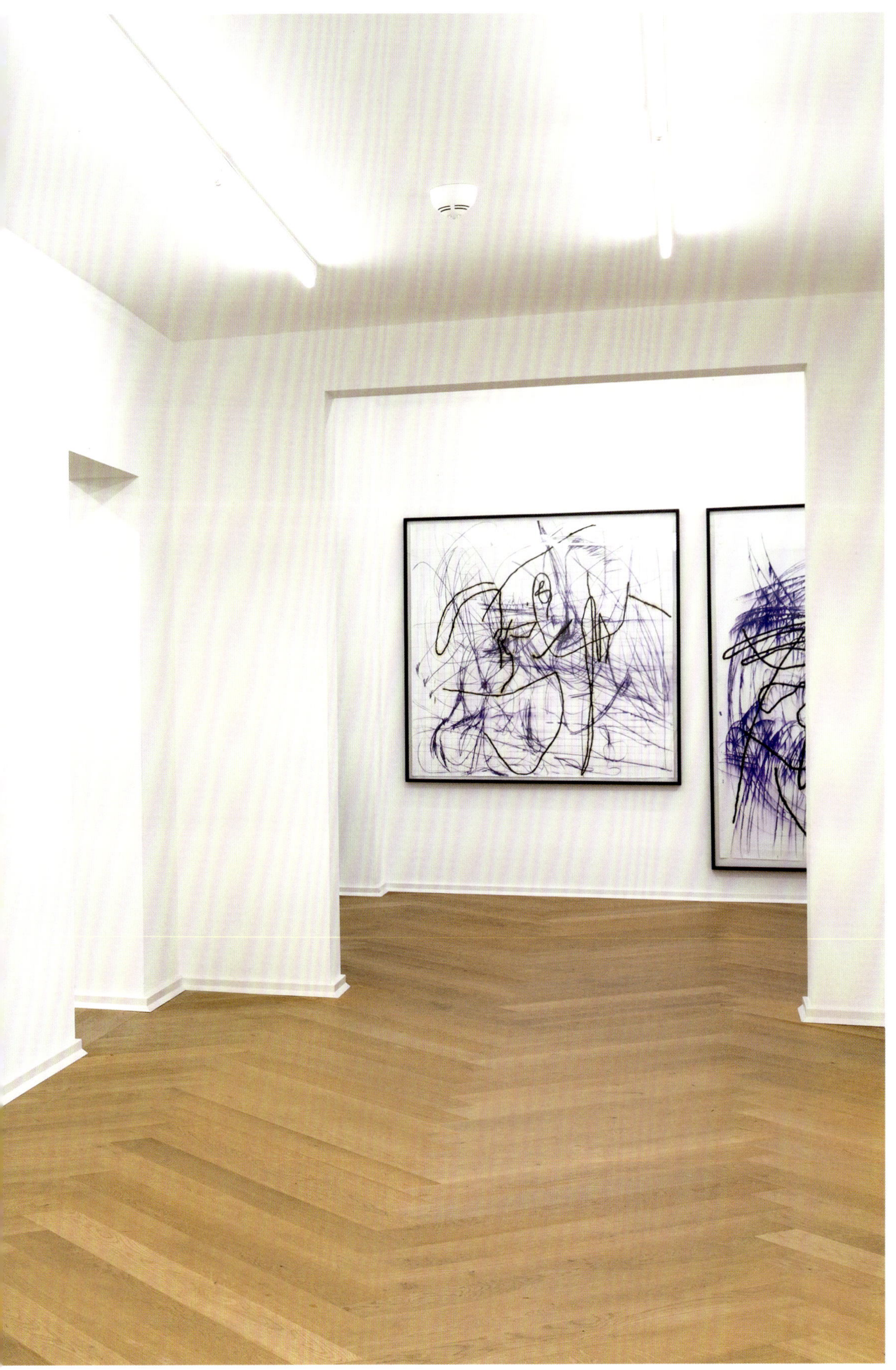

Dennoch sind Deine Bilder extrem körperlich. Sind die Bilder auch immer Zeichen Deiner eigenen Erfahrung? Die Hand, die zeichnend den Körper anwesend sein lässt? Die malerische Geste als Spur menschlicher Gegenwart?

**Besonders die »Spontacts« waren das, die Schwünge entsprachen oft meiner Armlänge. Und die Moves der Handschrift sind natürlich unmittelbar physisch. Gerade deshalb gilt es dann, es hinzukriegen, die Bilder zu objektivieren. Aber den Mensch kriegste kaum raus …**

Einige der »Specshifts« sind auch ohne figürliche Motive ganz schön ›fleischlich‹. Weniger Soutine und de Kooning, mehr Eiscafé Venezia Gelato-mäßig, später Guston, so ungefähr …

**Die hab' ich doch alle gern. Mein all-time favourite ist allerdings Pistazie. Aber klar, die werden aktuell wieder ›physischer‹.**

Als Du mit dem Studium fertig warst, befanden wir uns mitten in der letzten Wirtschaftskrise. Zehn Jahre später sieht's wieder so aus. Wie hält man sich zwischen den Krisen bei Laune?

**Bei letzten Mal hatte ich noch Jugendbonus und die Wirtschaft war mir komplett egal. Heute ist das anders, aber bis die Welt völlig im Eimer ist, halte ich hier einfach die Stellung.**

*Kadlites H3*, 2017
Acryl, Grafit und Blei auf Holz / Acrylic, graphite, and lead on canvas
140 × 104 cm / 55.1 × 40.9 in.

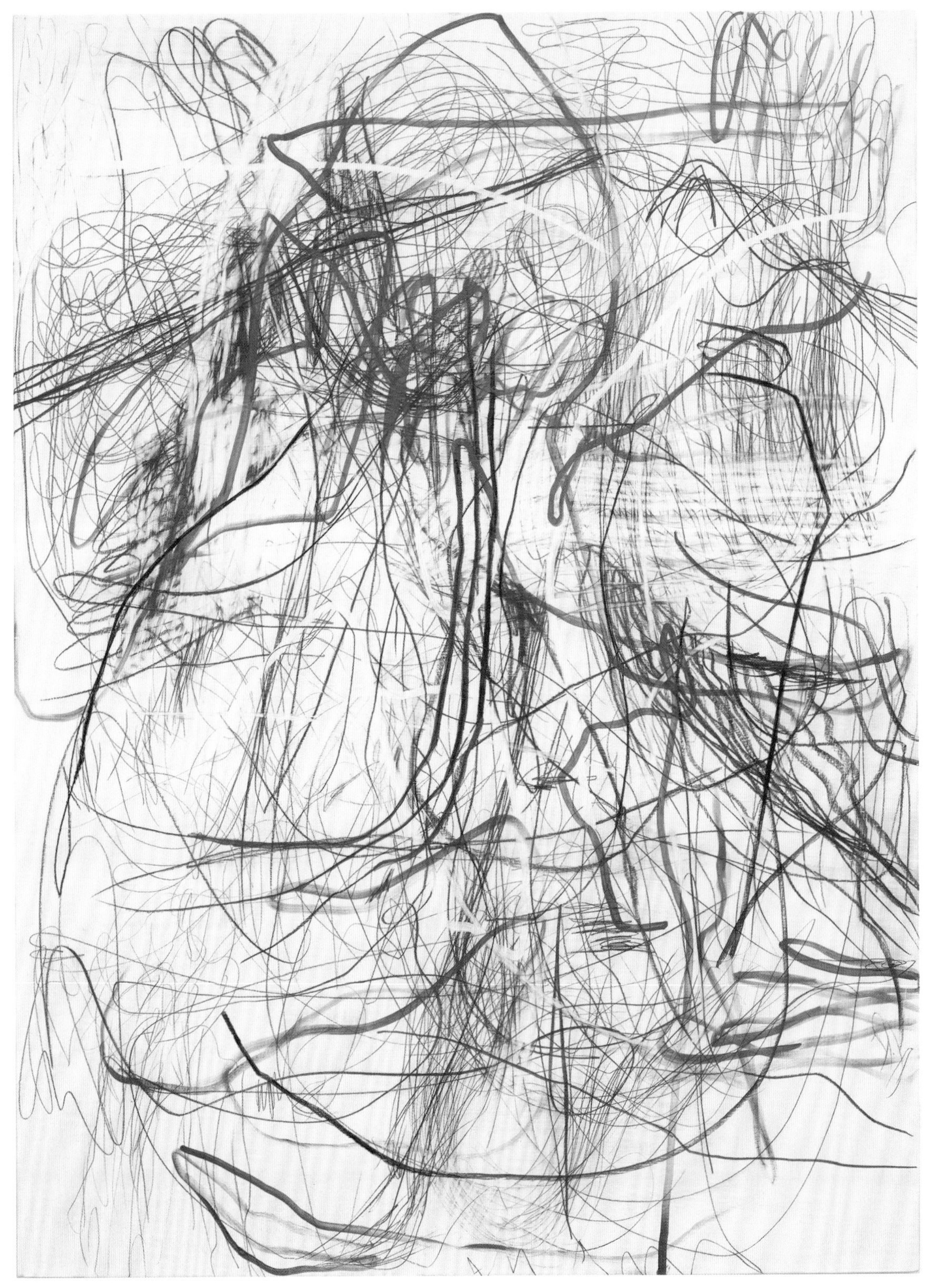

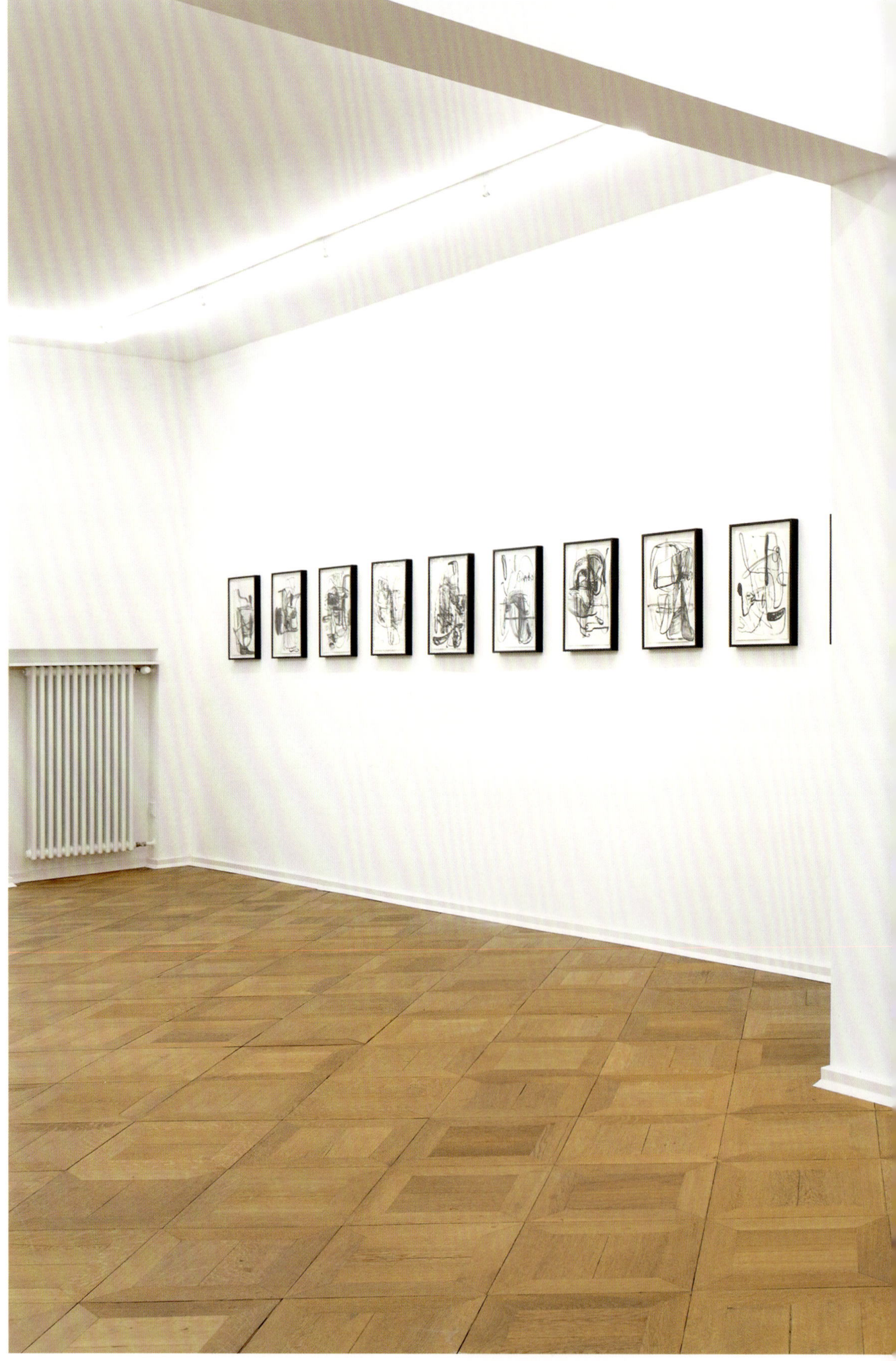

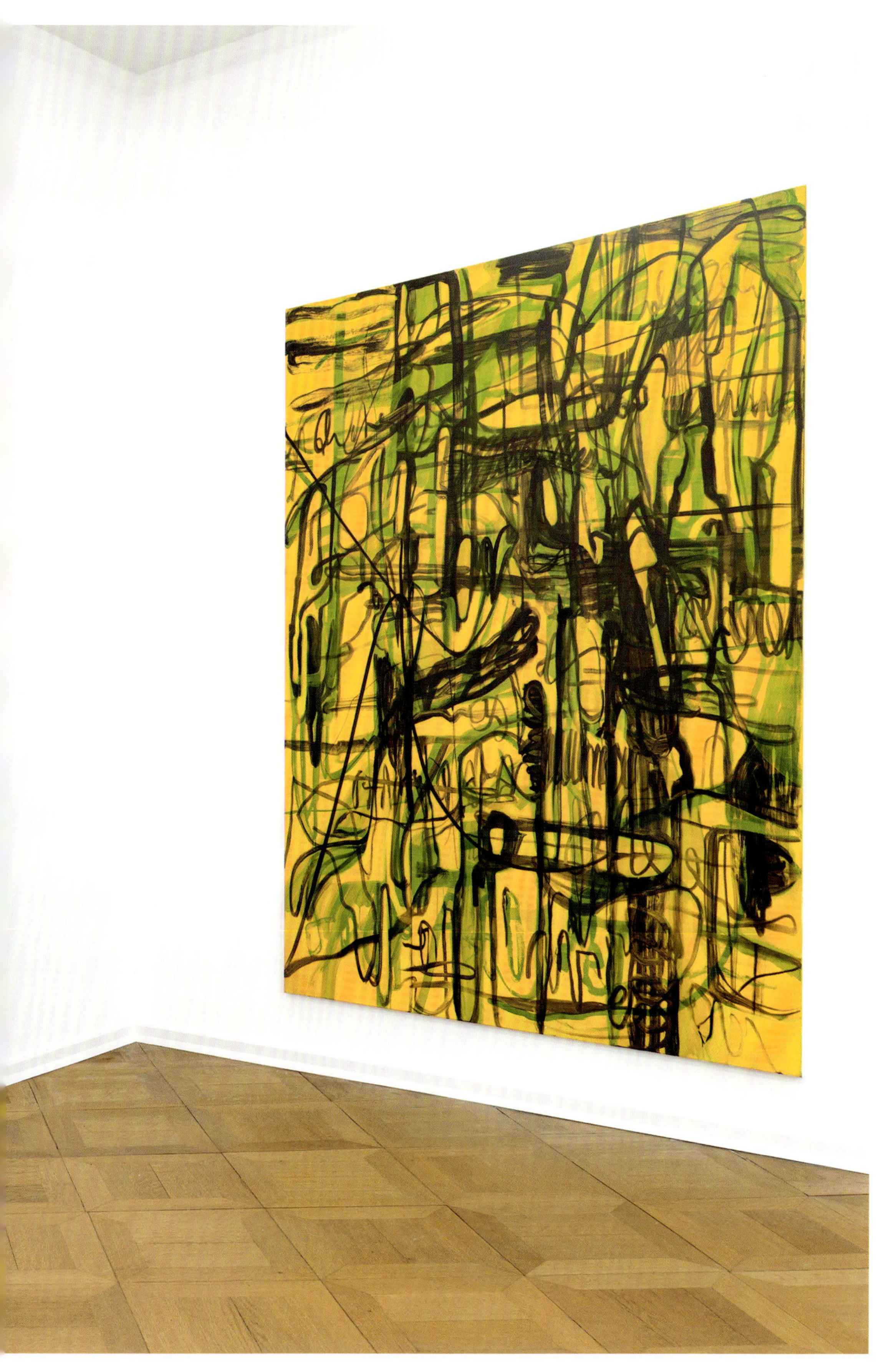

# Reset, Desire for Layers, Gelato

*Jana Schröder in Dialogue with Christian Malycha*

The title of your exhibition is "The Early Years." Is the "bonus of youth" already gone?

**Definitely! That's gone by the age of twenty-eight.**

In front of your paintings, what do we see? What's the story?

**There's no story.**

So form and content are the same?

**In every series, I have to deal with my personal pictorial questions: What does the familiar movement of handwriting do? Is it mostly about speed? What happens when my handwriting becomes illegible? How is it possible to integrate the aesthetics of diagrams? What happens if I only have two layers? What happens if additional layers are suddenly added, and new possibilities, say, eliminating particular things, come to mind? What happens when the meshes of paint are applied so densely that it becomes visually difficult to visually dissect the whole into its individual elements? Eventually, is all the "scrawling" able to create one whole? OK, things like that.**

One wouldn't suspect that your pictures were so rigorously structured and conceived.

**I strongly hope it doesn't unpleasantly strike people, in the first place!**

What then happens to the handwriting when it becomes illegible? What fascinates you about diagrams? Do you prefer to set or to break rules?

**Handwriting was simply a tool I used. I had trained the movement of my hand for such a long time that I could use it very intuitively, quite casually and naturally. That's the contrast I wanted to generate in opposition to the very deliberate lines in oil paint.**
**The aesthetics of scribbling are also quite beautiful. Something similar happens with the diagrams, in which even more scrawling, bustling, and arrows appear and create some sort of references. I've never understood diagrams, only got a headache from them, but they do look mind-bogglingly good. Apart from that, as a result of the appended grid structure, they form an additional third level in the "Spontacts" that makes it possible to conclude the first layer of copying pencil more clearly.**
**I enjoy setting rules just as much as I enjoy breaking them. Every broken rule becomes a new, adapted rule afterwards.**

Now, you're showing works from the past ten years and there are chronological chapters. What kinds of pictures did you select?

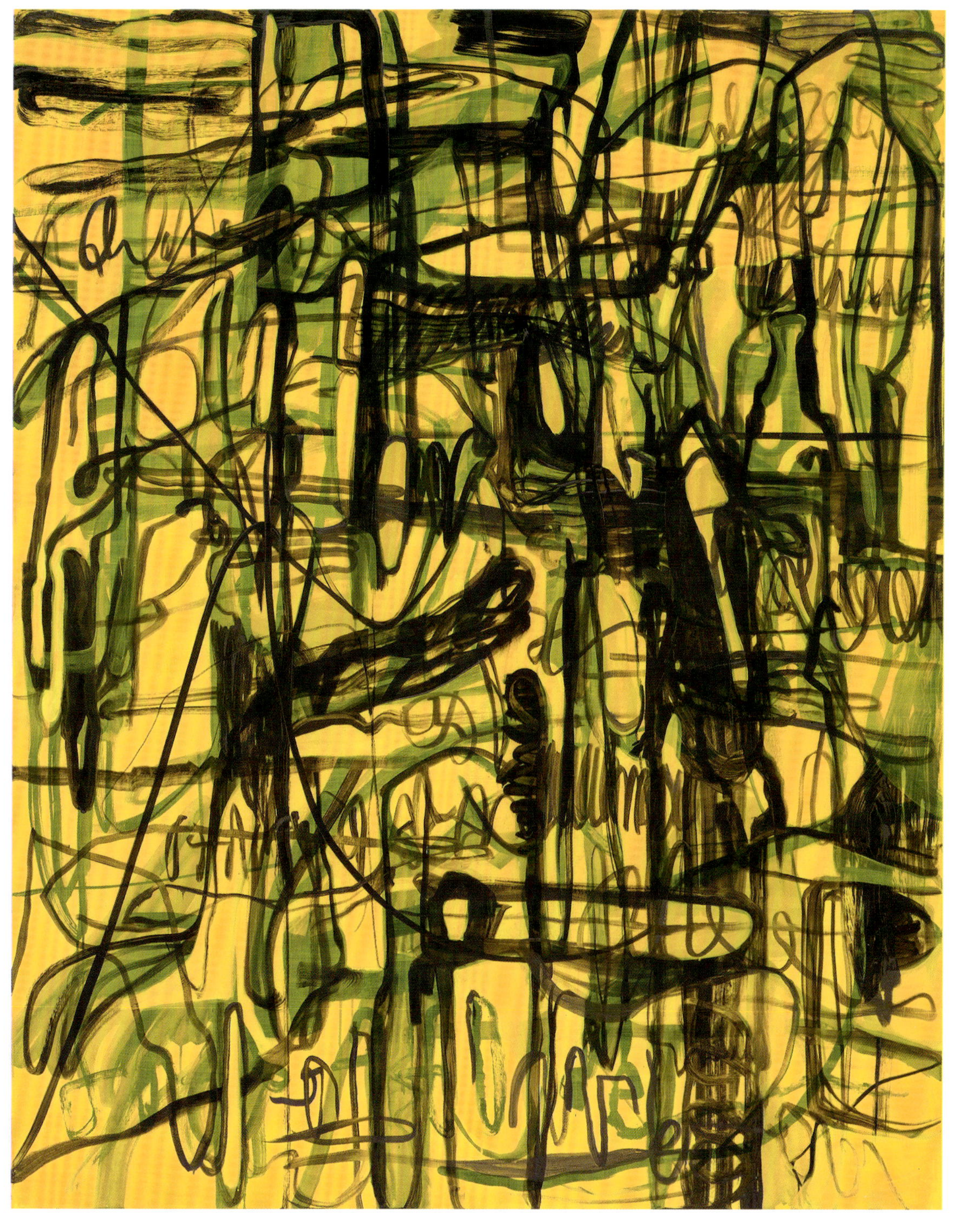

*Kadlites M18*, 2019
Acryl und Grafit auf Leinwand / Acrylic and graphite on canvas
200 × 160 cm / 78.7 × 63 in.

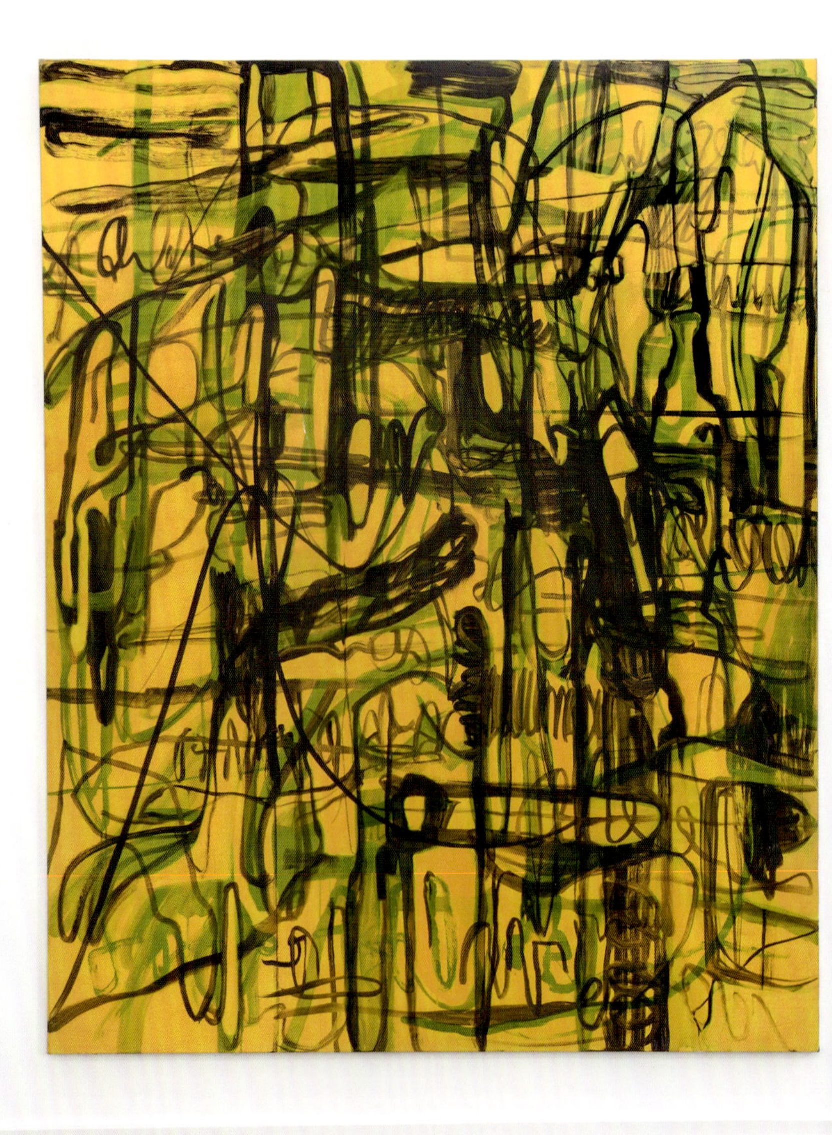

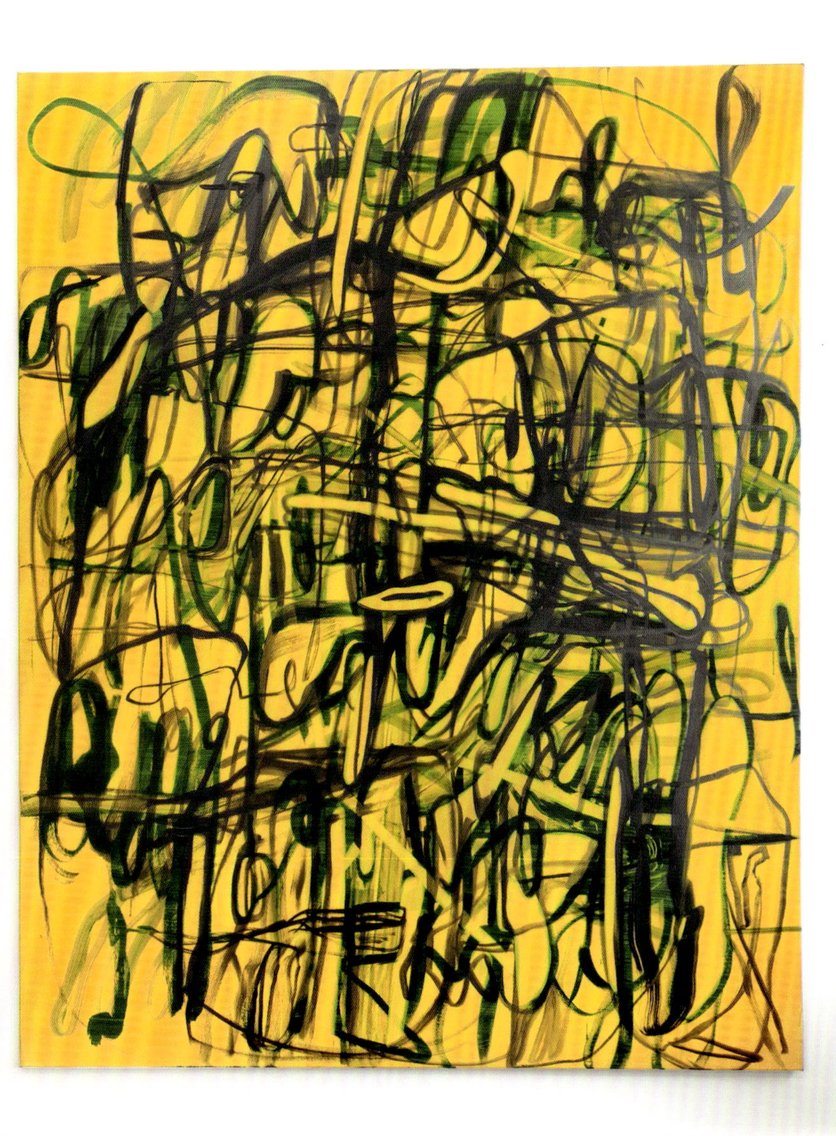

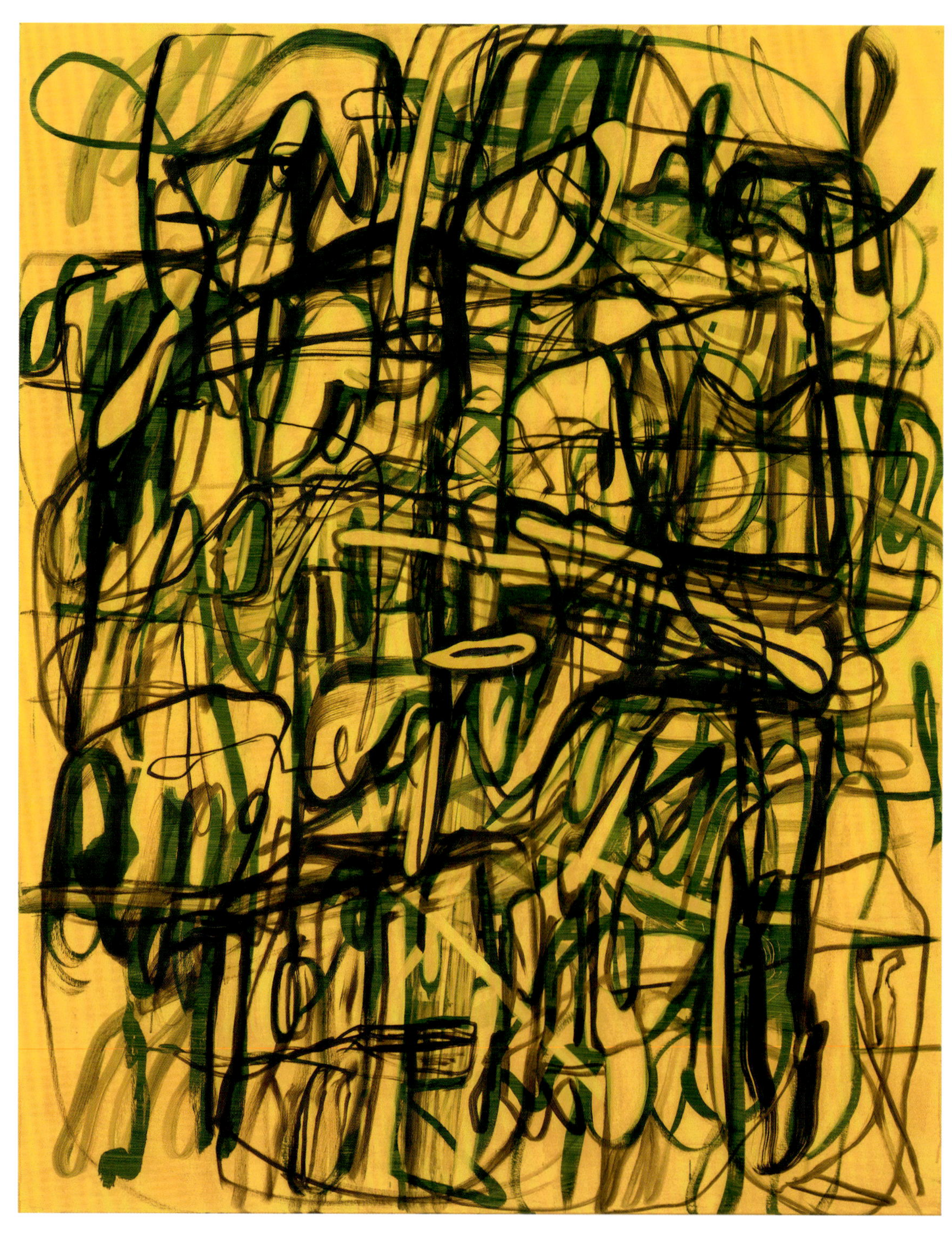

***Kadlites M15***, 2019
Acryl und Grafit auf Leinwand / Acryl an graphite on canvas
200 × 160 cm / 78.7 × 63 in.

**It begins with a painting from the "Kinkrustations" series. The "Spontacts" have their own room with blue-tinted windowpanes. Some of them already hung in the exhibition we did at Kunstverein Reutlingen. Back then bottom edges, now top edges. You have to be flexible, haven't you ... There are three "Kadlites" with very different approaches, but also two earlier, rather untypical ones on wooden panels, differing quite a bit from the later ones.**

However, the exhibition is only partially a retrospective. There are also very recent paintings and works on paper that have never been shown before.

**Yes, a few small works on paper are hung in between. I haven't done such small works for ages. They emerged when the "Kadlites" were finished, and that led to the entirely new "Neurosox." The last painting in the room with the fireplace is one of those. It's the only one I specifically painted for the exhibition and for this particular room.**
**I quite fancy that the new ones are hanging in between, since everything is mutually dependent on each other and things do always push themselves further.**

Diversity and connectedness?

**Isn't that lovely! Even I myself haven't seen them all together before.**

Self-examination and self-insecurity?

**I'm actually more of an advocate of not mixing different series. But at the foundation it works really well. Self-examination is therefore not really wrong. In addition, one always walks in a circle there, even several times . . . And nothing would come about at all without self-insecurity—that's always a neat thing.**

What about the various groups? You told me the first "Spontacts" were created as textual images. It's only that the gestures of handwriting immediately turn into gestural figures, text becomes texture. How did that come about?

**In the very first "Spontacts," there really are a couple of letters, mostly upside down or mirrored, sometimes also with wrong spelling. But as it was never about text in the sense of a reference, the paintings became illegible very quickly.**

While the "Spontacts" seem almost immaterial, the "Kinkrustations" are the extreme opposite of them: massive and hermetic, heavy and dense. You quite clearly needed a contrast to the openness and lightness of the "Spontacts".

**Exactly! Both series were created at the same time and even the "Kinkrustations" are primarily concerned with lines. But that's much more difficult to decipher than in the "Spontacts." It's sometimes no longer comprehensible at all. There are different speeds: intentional acceleration, deliberate deceleration.**

Lines that disperse and lines that become concentrated?

**That's the thing.**

Both series came to an end in 2017 and you then created the first "Kadlites."

**I started working on the "Kadlites" as early as 2011. I just set them aside. Yet, the blue of the "Spontacts" was eventually so fair that I was finally ready to continue working with that profane yellow.**

Why yellow?

**Well, yellow is a really dumb color. Nonetheless, it was the only color capable of the translucent passages I wanted to have. It absorbs something, but also still allows enough to come forth.**

That's the appeal?

**The "Spontacts" almost exclusively have only two layers: copying pencil and then oil paint on the copying pencil. I had no chance at all to correct anything. At least not by blotting something out or making something disappear visually. You see everything on the white canvas. The "correction" consisted more of countering the errors in the layer of the copying pencil with the superimposed strokes of slowly applied oil. Or really emphasizing them. That was the task I set myself.**
**As I already mentioned, the "Ultra-Diagrams" with their three layers are a minimal exception.**
**After a while, I was then overcome with a downright desire for layers. One sees that the "Kadlites" can have up to seventeen layers. And I even indulged myself again in being able to "erase" things. The best thing about it is that the erased areas become something entirely of their own.**

This led to the "Neurosox" in 2019. Still, color disappears again, the paintings are black-and-white.

**That, I believe, was a reset.**

And suddenly, they became painterly.

**After scribbling around for such a long time, I really was up to painting. This already began with the last "Kadlites." The translucent parts covered many planes, but the corrected areas where lines had been erased were always planar surfaces. And as of a certain width of a line, one can ponder whether it's not really painting in any case.**

The gray is astonishing, since it is so cunningly nuanced, it constantly shifts the layers against each other and keeps renegotiating the pictorial balance.

**That's the lead powder. Most of the "Neurosox" are painted just with white paint and lead powder. Lead powder is indestructible. It gets everywhere. I like that.**

There's an even clearer shift in characteristics with the "Specshifts." How fundamental is that shift?

**I would prefer not to see any shift at all between the "Neurosox" and the "Specshifts." Both series are still in progress.**

The same thing? One black-and-white, the other in color?

**To a certain extent, yes. Color contrasts achieve something different than chiaroscuro. And thanks to color, I bring in even more painting at the same time.**

So far, there have been gestural drawings upon or in front of a colorful ground. The "Specshifts" are not only chromatic, but structured by contrasts. The relationships between the colors are much more complex. That reminds me of paintings you did at the academy . . .

**Yes, me too . . . After the "Spontacts," I already resumed something I had done before, and made the link to the yellow. That was possible because the "Kadlites" hadn't been thought through before. It was similar afterwards. To develop something new, I initially allowed a lot of things. Things sometimes go wrong in the process. The previous works worked, methodically and stringently, but then all the doors are suddenly opened again and all possibilities are back. It's first necessary to sort that out.**

In the "Neurosox" and "Specshifts," the graphic textures become an interwoven fabric with a huge breadth and depth.

**The layers do now also get all tangled up. Breadth and depth didn't interest me in the past. They actually bothered me. I've never even once painted over the edge or treated the entire surface in the same way. Now I'll soon probably have to pay a bit more attention again.**
**Since, if I now add a couple more colors, the question that naturally arises is which of the old rules and routines still remain. Some things which previously worked really well don't work at all anymore. But other things do work again and indeed work really well.**

The new pictures are quite stunning. Do they captivate you, too?

**Unfortunately, I have to admit, they do, like a raging river!**

Summarizing the past ten years: Line becomes planar. Chiaroscuro unfolds chromatic contrasts. The graphic becomes painterly. Pictorial fields become pictorial spaces. Is that accurate?

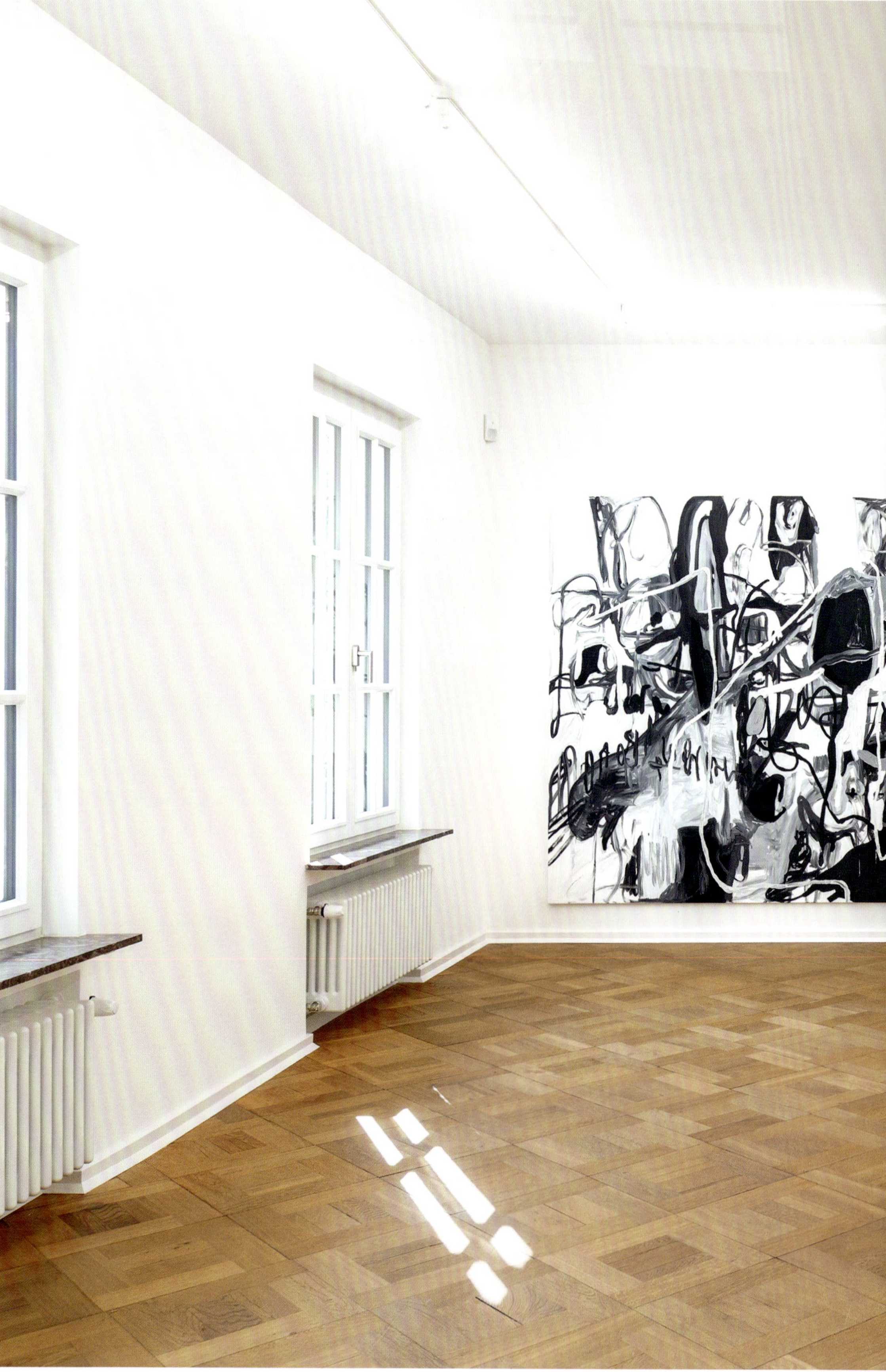

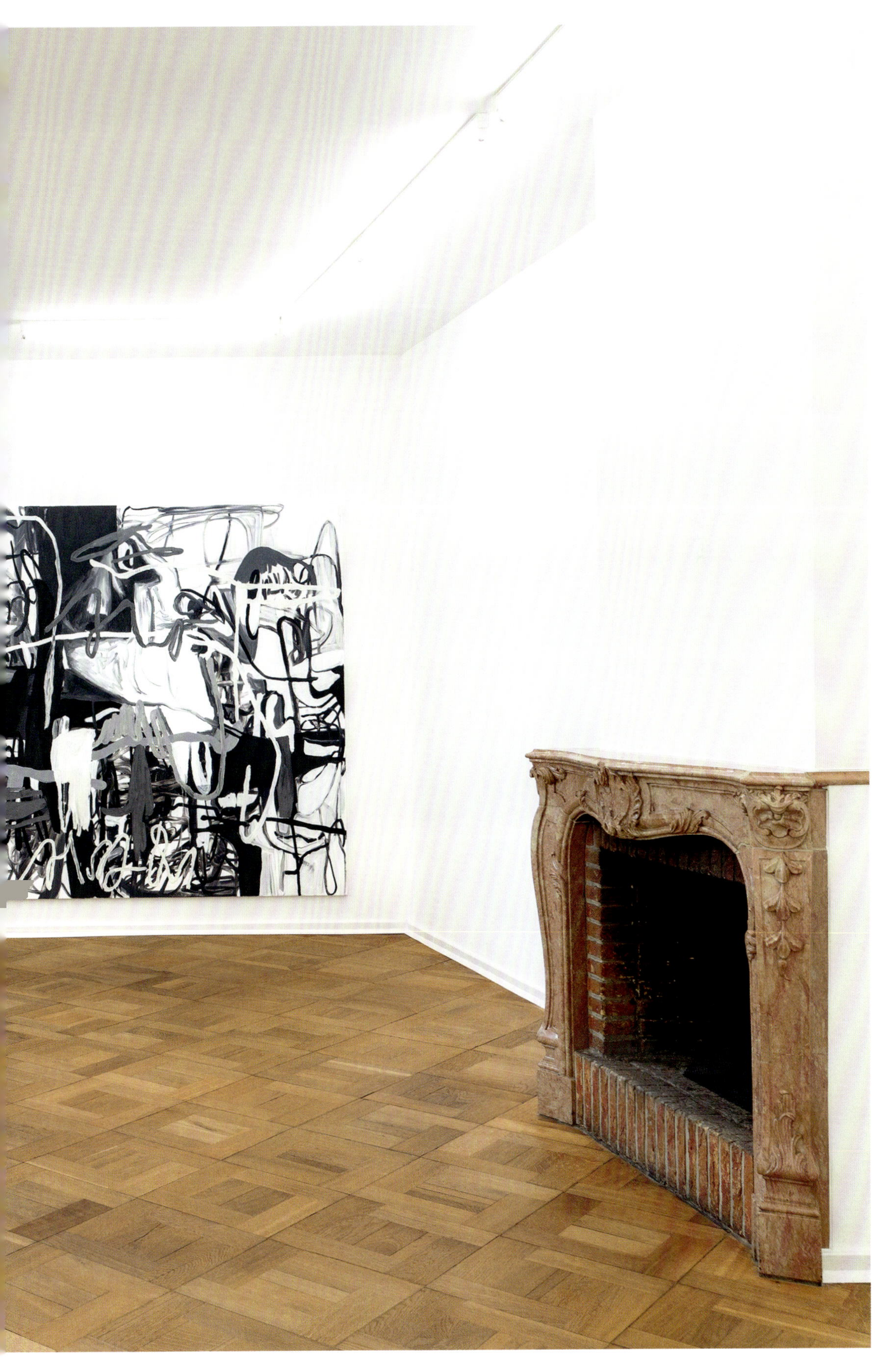

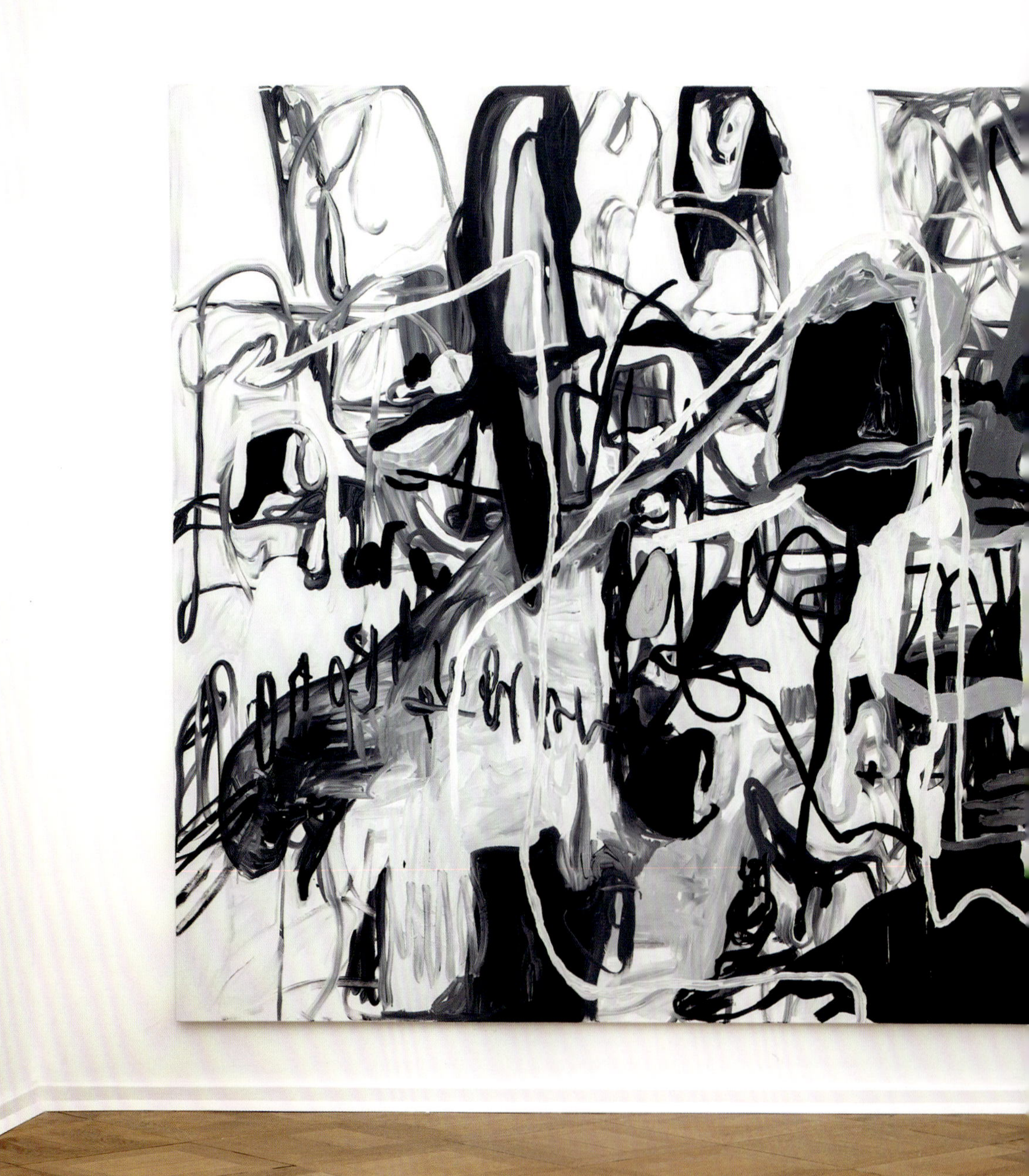

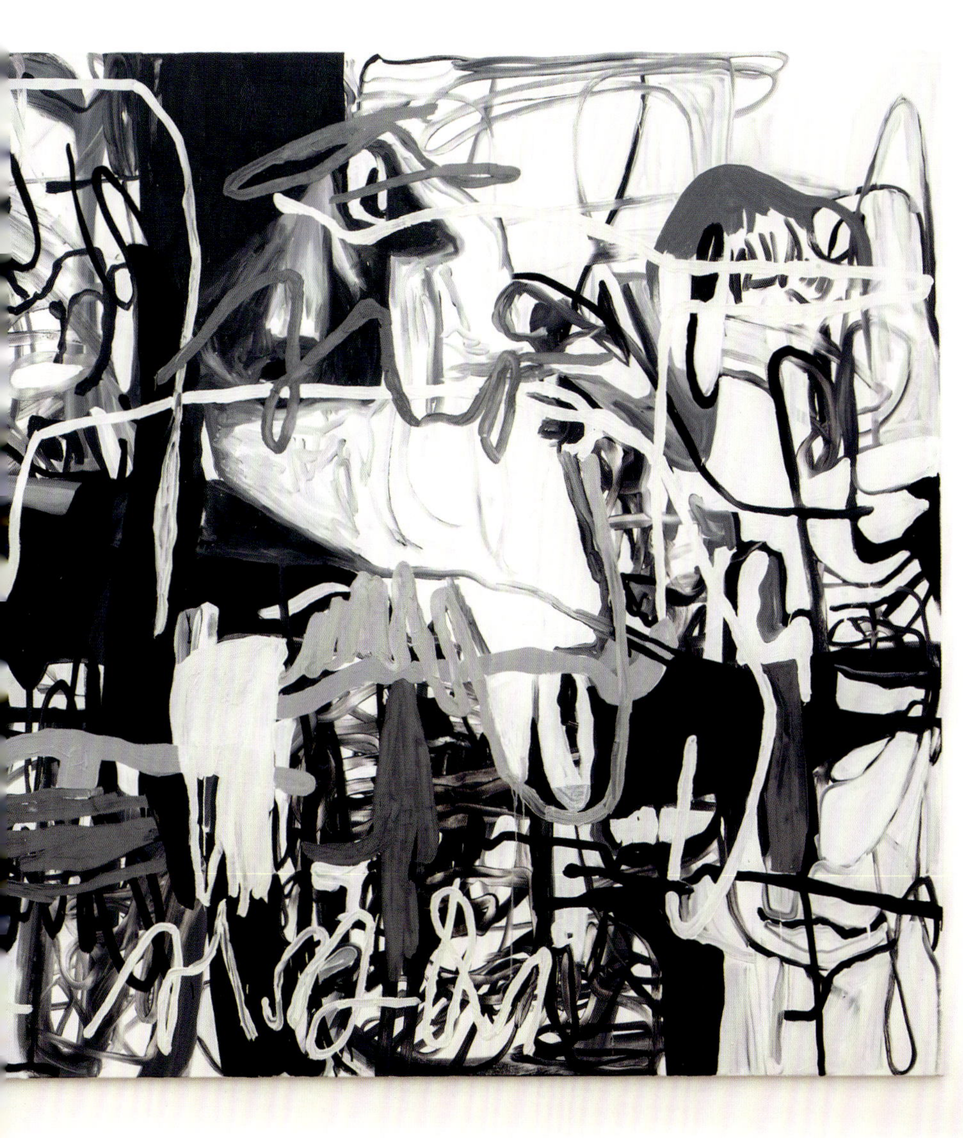

**Certainly.**

How do you recognize a finished painting?

**I always work on several pictures at the same time. When something has been standing in the studio for a couple of days and I don't find anything in need of alteration, it's finished.**

Nonetheless, it sometimes seems to me as if your paintings are always in the middle of an indefinite movement, always between coming and going, emerging and vanishing.

**It seems that way to me, too. I'm very distracted and that's also getting worse and worse.**

You work in series, you always have and done so consistently. Even the formats have remained relatively constant over the years. Nevertheless, every picture is distinctive and individual.

**The formats are the same because I'm lazy. 240 × 200 cm is big enough and still easy enough to move. Smaller is generally more difficult, and bigger always works well. Then comes the fact that I'm a blunt kind of person and always prefer or seem to tolerate it better when several paintings of the same format hang next to each other. Their differences then also become more visible, clearer, from one image to the next in a series. I've always found out something different in every painting and the outliers frequently are the most fruitful.**

How "expressive," how "conceptual" are your paintings?

**I think there's a balance. If an expressive gesture remains, it's automatically part of the approach. Generally, I start expressively . . . Though I would actually prefer to avoid the word and replace it with: things generally start brutishly ... and all the decisions that follow narrow things down and become more and more intentional.**

Your paintings are nevertheless extremely physical. Are they an indication of your own experience? The hand that makes the body present while drawing? The painterly gesture as a trace of human presence?

**The "Spontacts" were that way, since the sweeps often corresponded to the length of my arm. The moves of my hand are, of course, directly physical as well. That's why it was then necessary to objectify the pictures. But it's almost impossible to be done with the human quality . . .**

Still, some of the "Specshifts" are pretty "fleshy" even without a figurative motif. Not so much Soutine and de Kooning, rather Venice ice cream parlor gelato-like, late Guston ...

**Of course, I adore all of them, naturally. Anyhow, my all-time favorite is pistachio. But the paintings definitely are becoming more "physical" right now.**

By the end of your studies, we found ourselves in the middle of the last economic crisis. Ten years later, it looks that way again. How does one keep up the good spirits between crises?

**The last time, I still had the bonus of youth and business didn't mean anything to me. Things are different today, but until the world finally goes down the drain, I'll simply hold the fort.**

*Kadlites M5*, 2017
Acryl, Grafit, Blei und Öl auf Leinwand / Acrylic, graphite, lead, and oil on canvas
200 × 155 cm / 78.7 × 61 in.

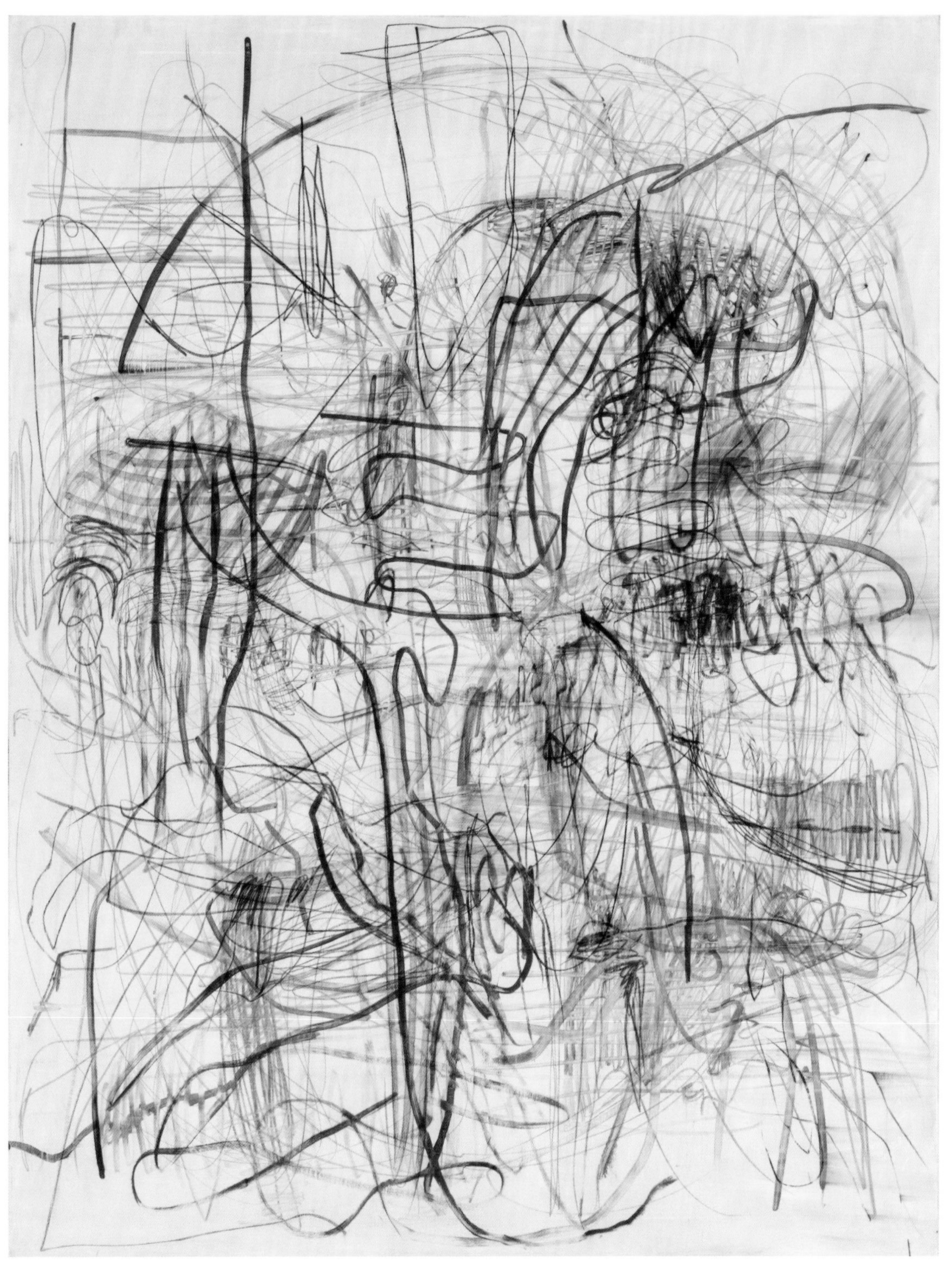

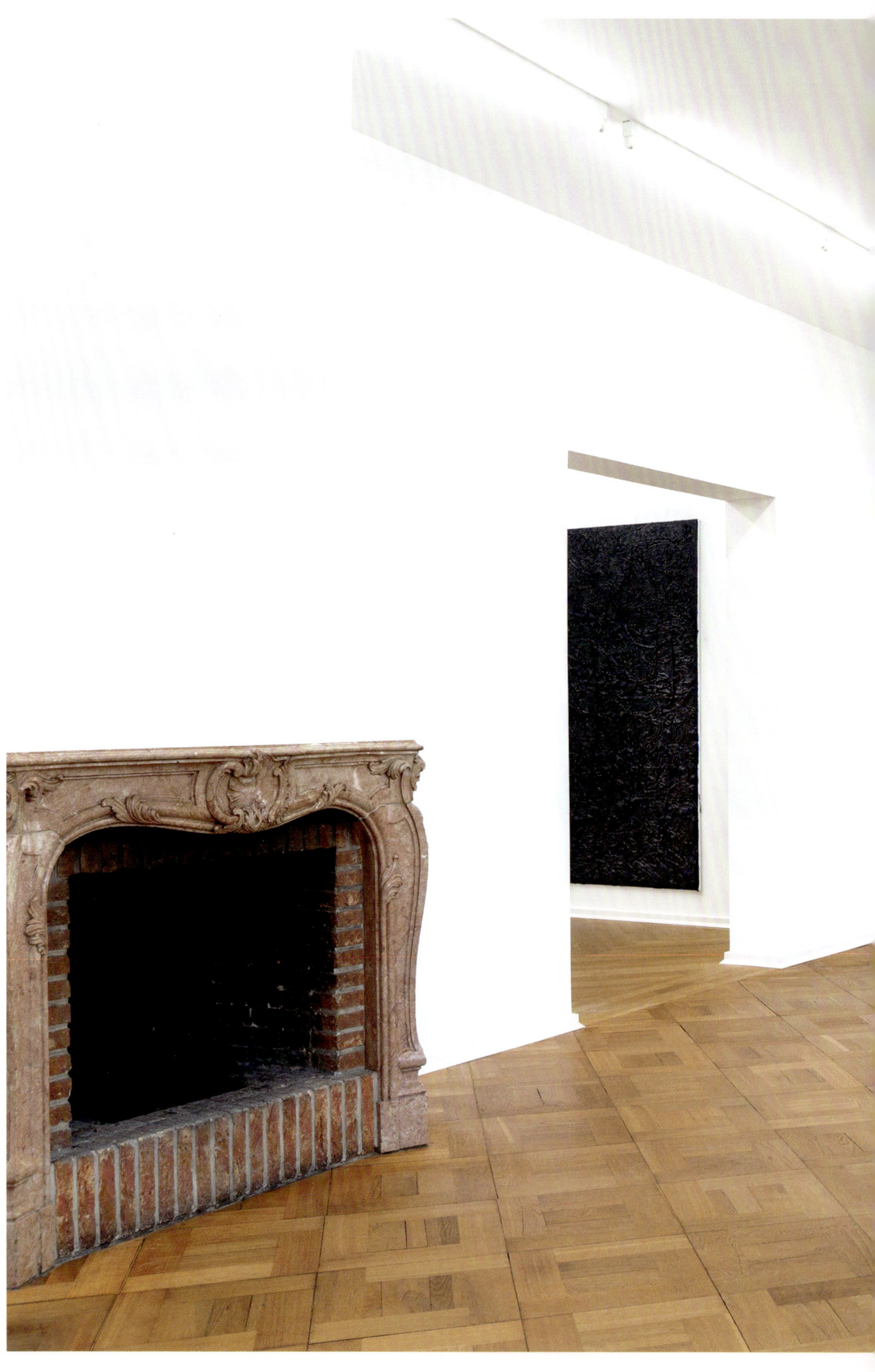

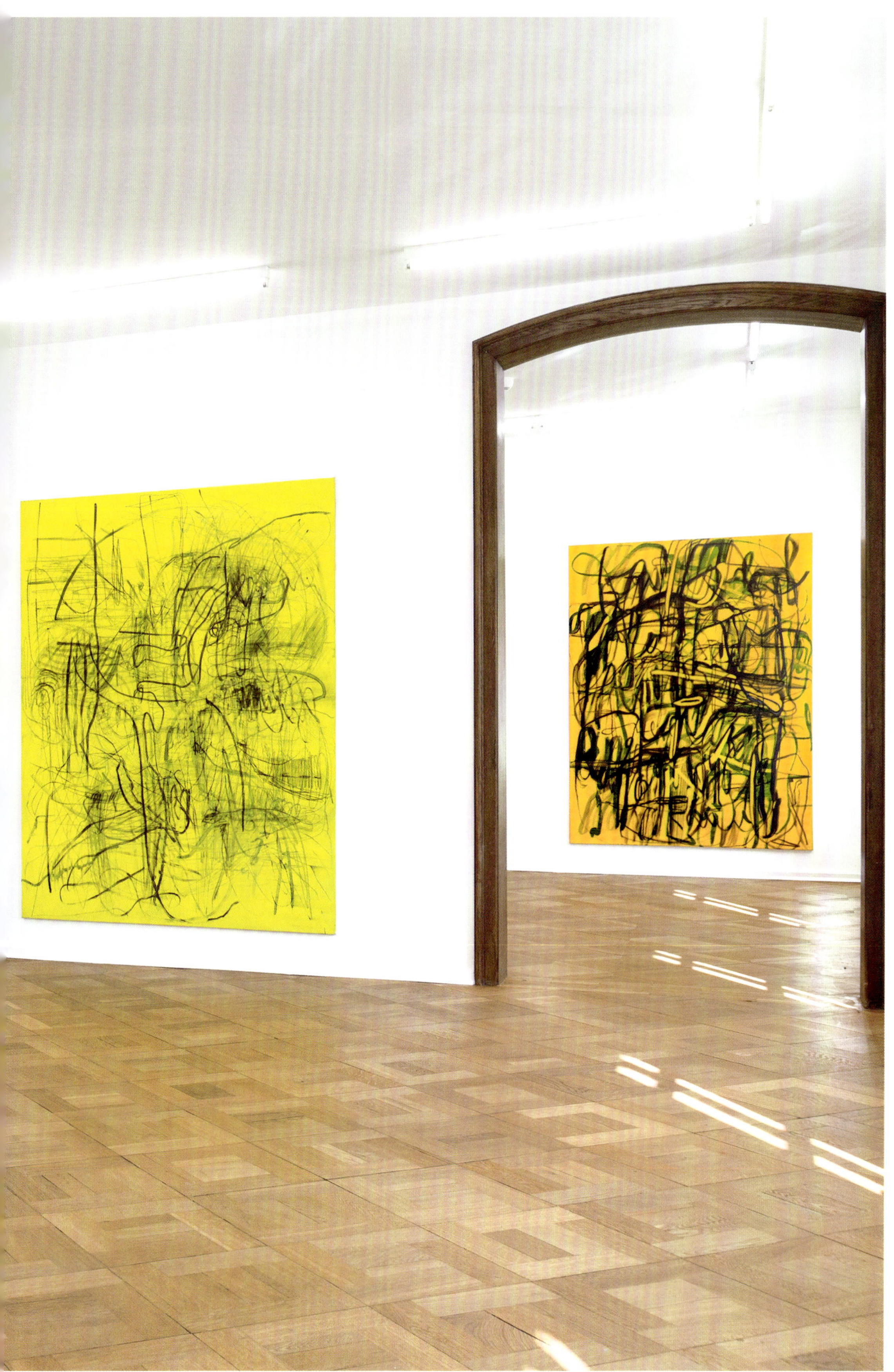

## JANA SCHRÖDER

1983 Geboren / Born in Brilon

2005 – 2009 Kunstakademie Düsseldorf (Klasse / class Albert Oehlen)

**Ausgewählte Einzelausstellungen / Selected solo exhibitions**

2020 *Jana Schröder - The Early Years*, Kopfermann-Fuhrmann Stiftung, Düsseldorf
2019 *Kadlites RS6-17*, T293 Gallery, Rom / Rome
*Kadlites*, Nino Mier Gallery, Los Angeles
2018 *Vote*, Kunstverein Heppenheim (mit / with Andreas Breunig)
*ECCO Gelb*, ANMO Art CHA, Düsseldorf (mit / with Maurizio Nannucci)
*Kadlites and Kinkrustations*, Natalia Hug Gallery, Köln / Cologne
2017 *Spontacts and Kinkrustations*, Kunstverein Reutlingen
2016 *Spontacts FX*, T293 Gallery, Rome
*Spontacts/The Ultra-Diagram Series*, Natalia Hug Gallery, Köln / Cologne
2015 *Spontacts*, Nino Mier Gallery, Los Angeles

**Ausgewählte Gruppenausstellungen / Selected group exhibitions**

2020 *Echo Chambers*, Galerie Bärbel Grässlin, Frankfurt am Main
*Paper (and one on wood)*, Nino Mier Gallery, Los Angeles
*Jetzt! Junge Malerei in Deutschland*, Deichtorhallen, Hamburg
2019 *Endless*, Natalia Hug Gallery, Köln / Cologne
*Jetzt! Junge Malerei in Deutschland*, Kunstmuseum Bonn, Museum Wiesbaden, Kunstsammlungen Chemnitz
*Painting Zeitgeist?*, Achenbach Hagemeier, Düsseldorf
2018 *Trance*, Aishti Foundation, Beirut
2017 *20cm from the ground*, L21 Gallery, Palma de Mallorca
*Quintessenz*, Galerie Guido W. Baudach, Berlin
*Group Show*, Natalia Hug Gallery, Köln / Cologne
2015 *Oh, of course you were berry picking*, DREI, Köln / Cologne
*Present Conditional*, Nino Mier Gallery, Los Angeles
*New Galerie @ Yves Klein Archives*, Yves Klein Archives, Paris
*Zombie Routine*, New Galerie, Paris
2014 *17 Abstract Paintings*, Wertheim, Köln / Cologne
*Hausreste*, Haus der Kunst Sankt Josef, Solothurn
*L'aventura – Die mit der Liebe spielen*, Palazzo Guaineri delle Cossere, Brescia
2012 *Painting Show*, Galerie Berthold Pott, Köln / Cologne
2011 *Fine Line*, KIT Kunst im Tunnel, Düsseldorf

2019 – 2015

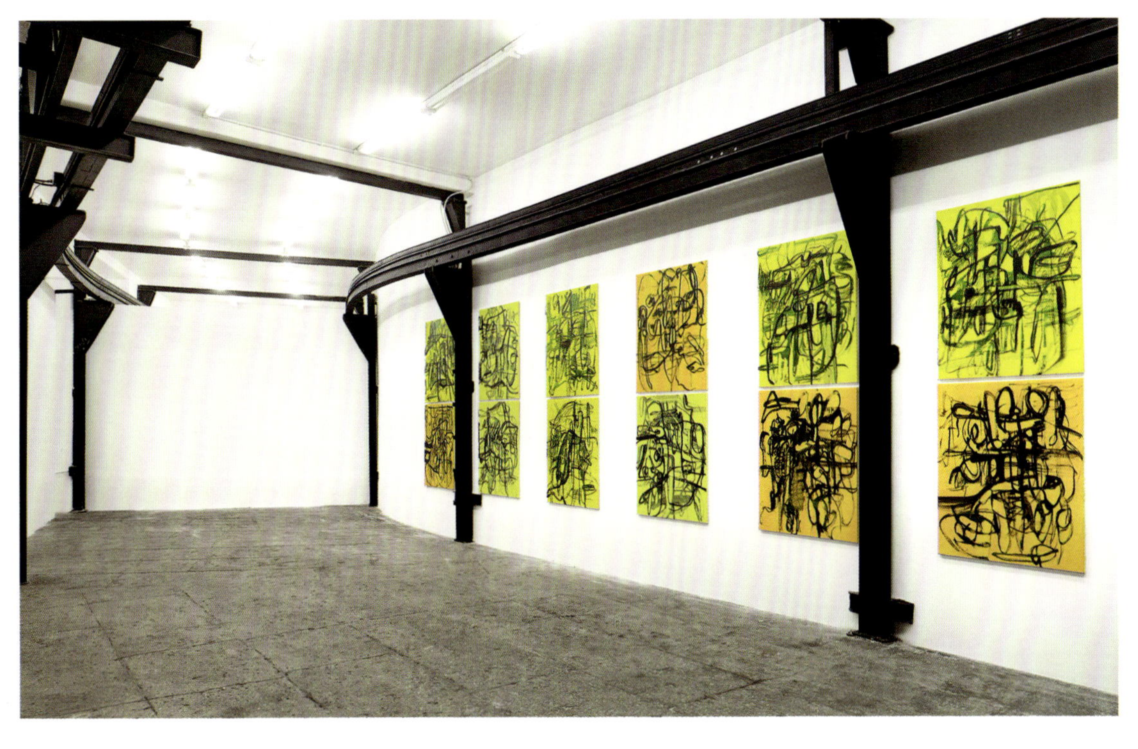

RS6-17, T293 Gallery, Rom / Rome, 2019

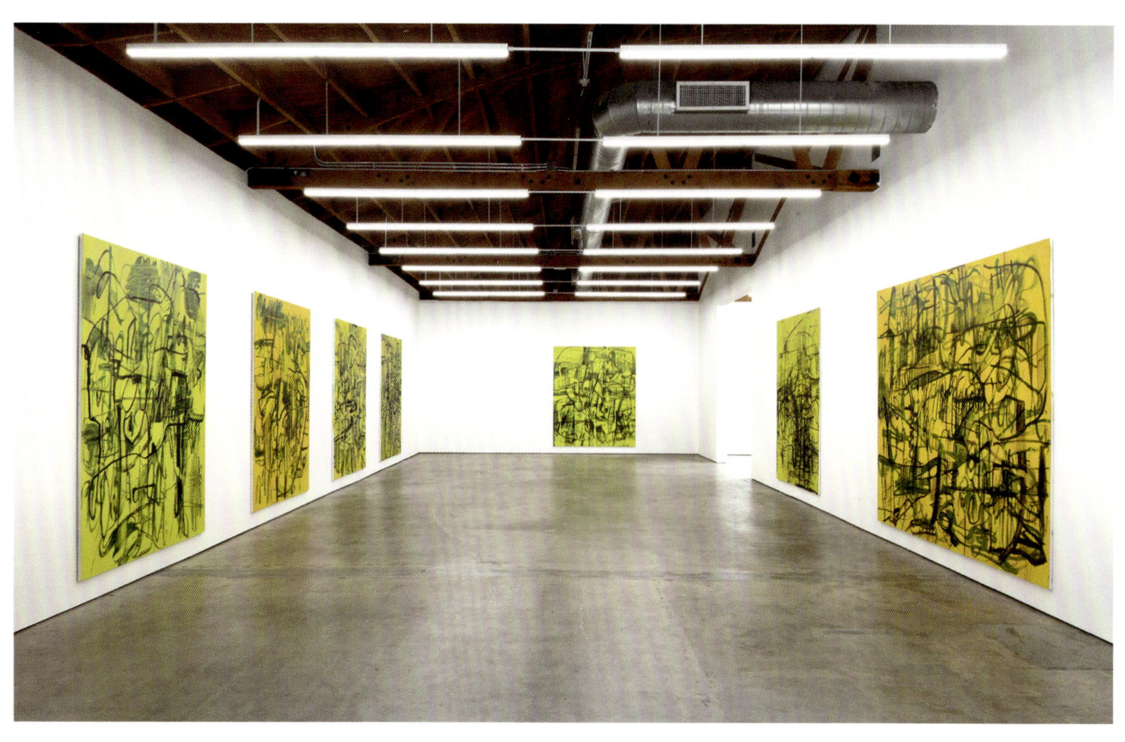

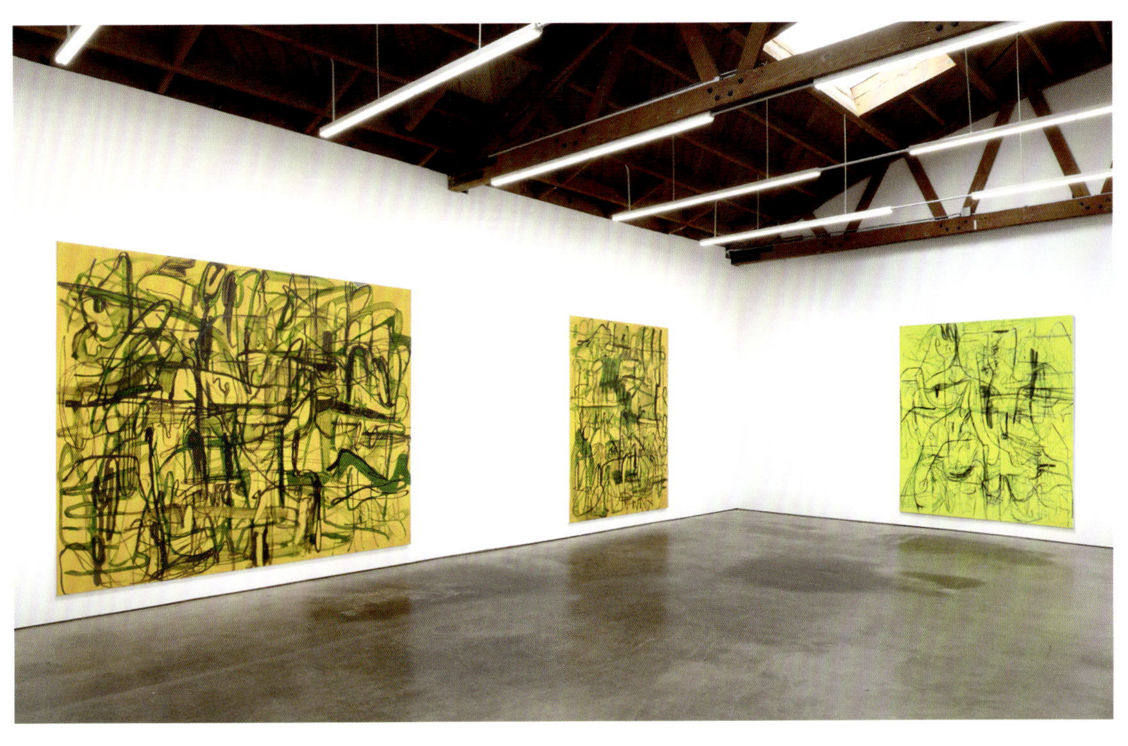

*Kadlites*, Nino Mier Gallery, Los Angeles, 2019

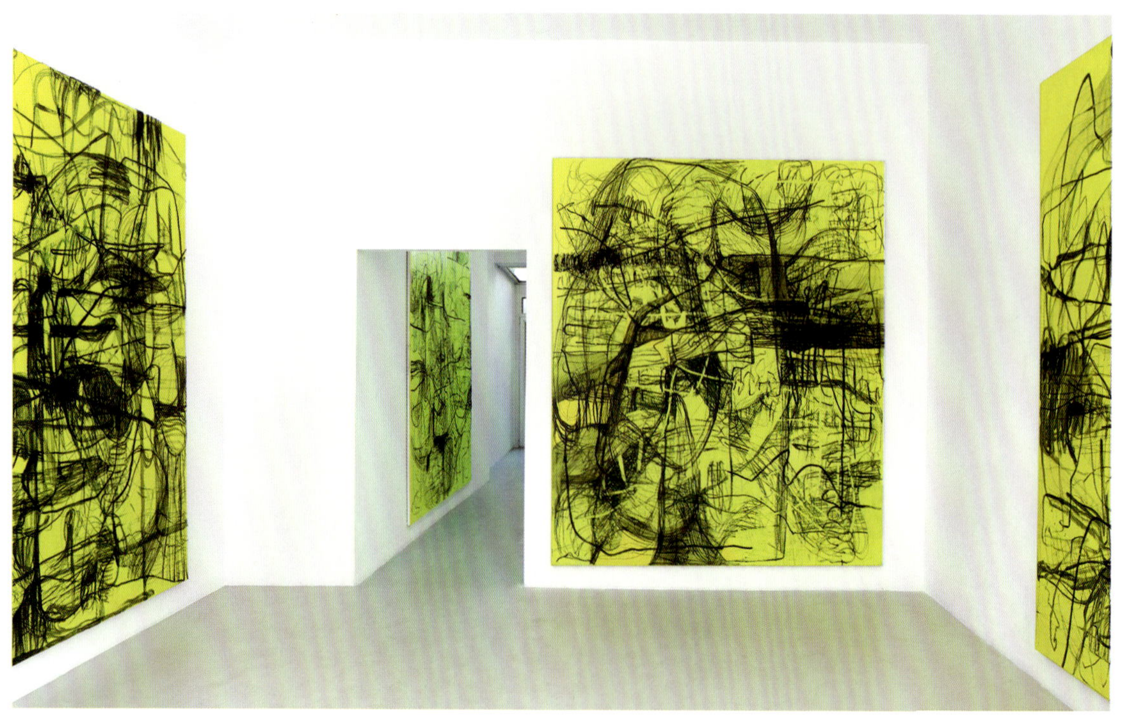

*Kadlites and Kinkrustations*, Natalia Hug Gallery, Köln / Cologne, 2018

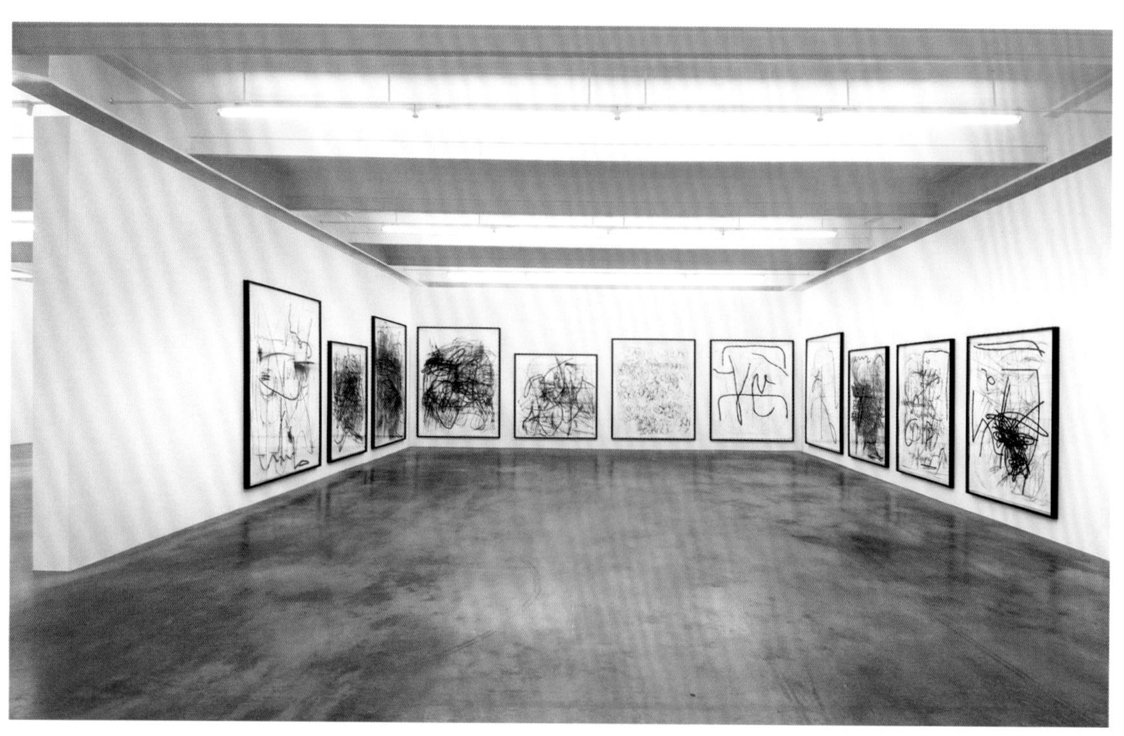

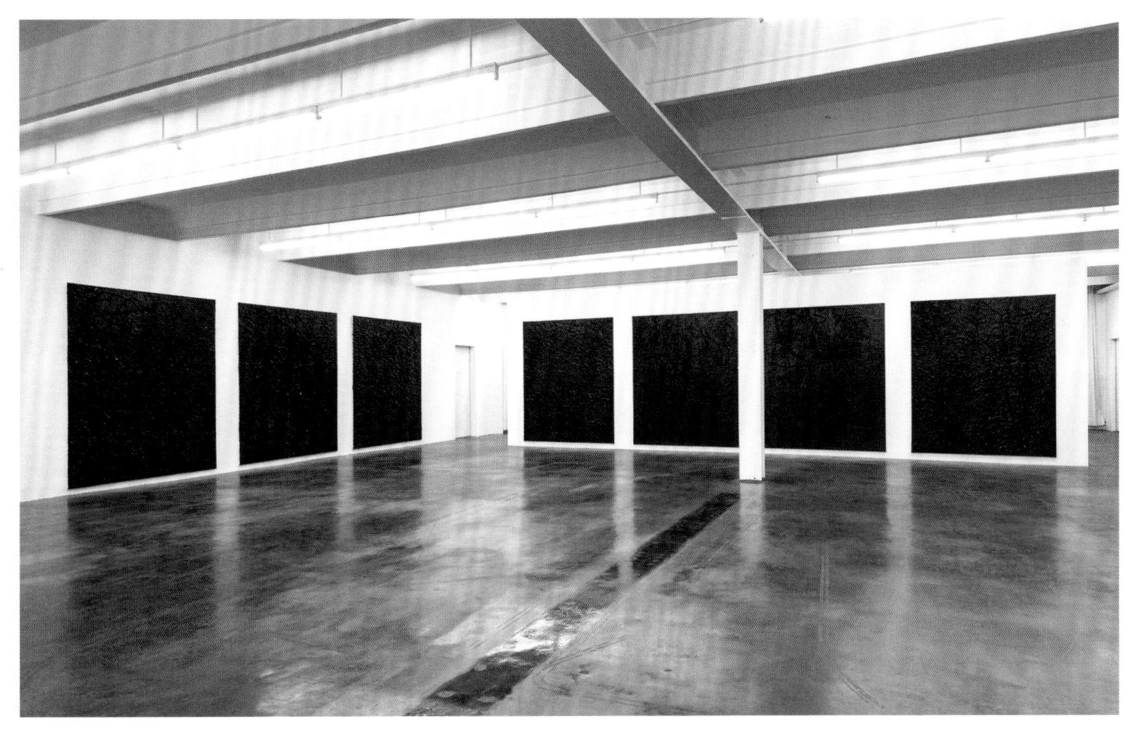

*Spontacts and Kinkrustations*, Kunstverein Reutlingen, 2017

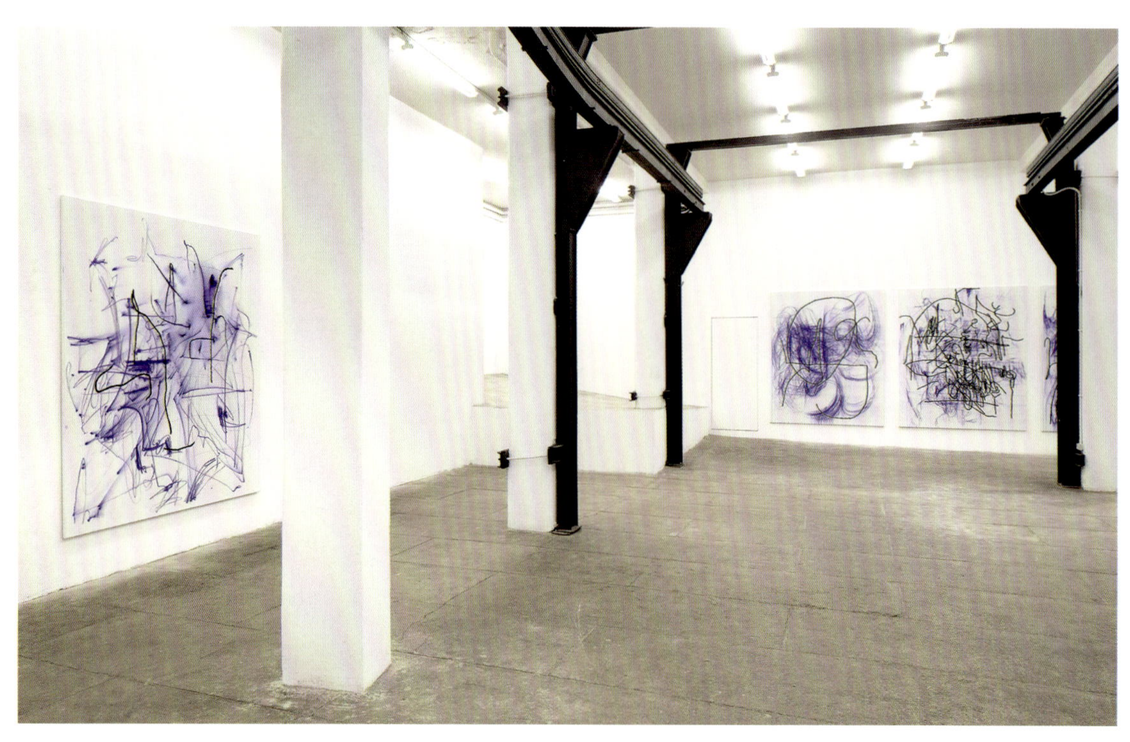

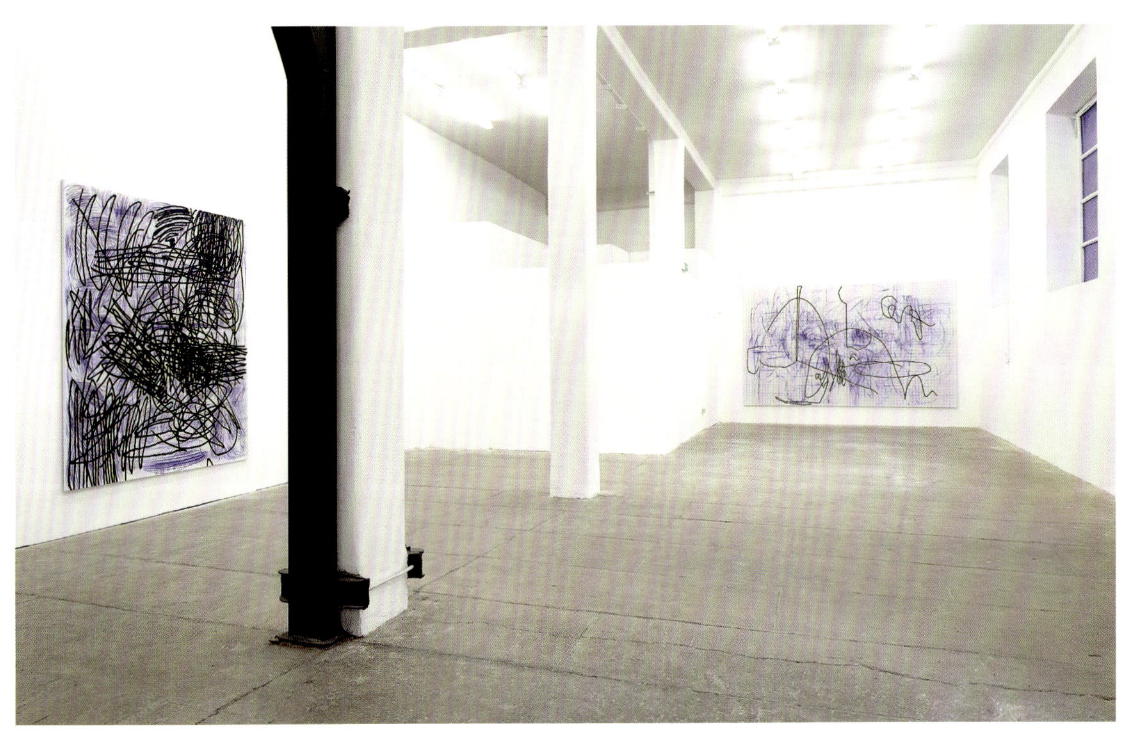

*Spontacts FX*, T293 Gallery, Rom / Rome, 2016

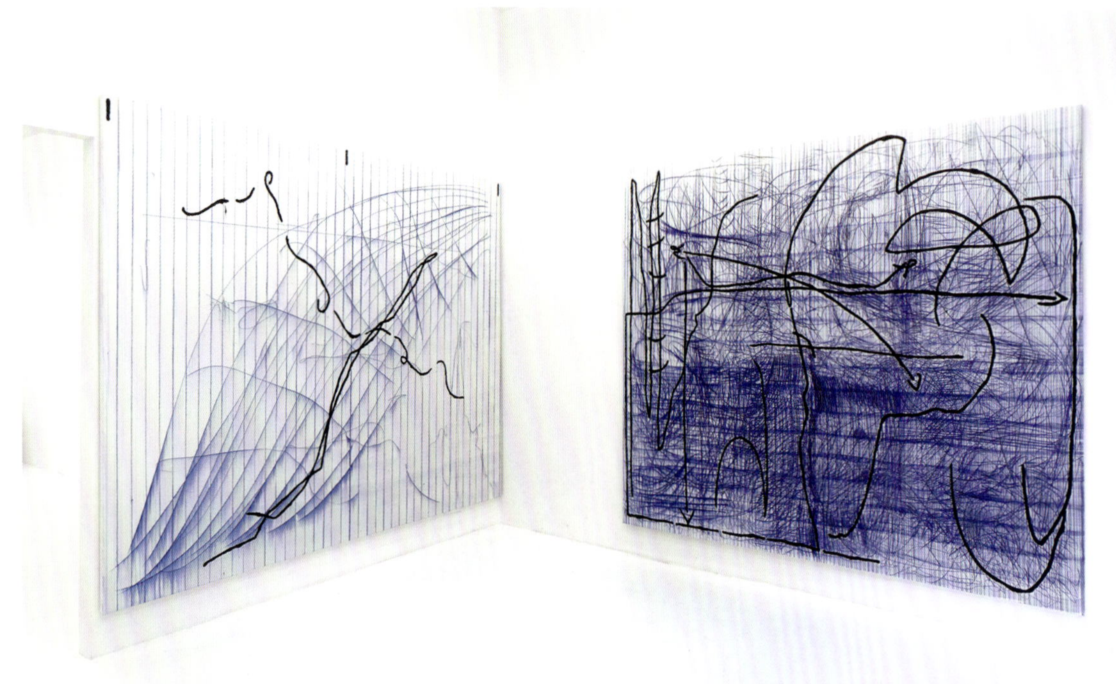

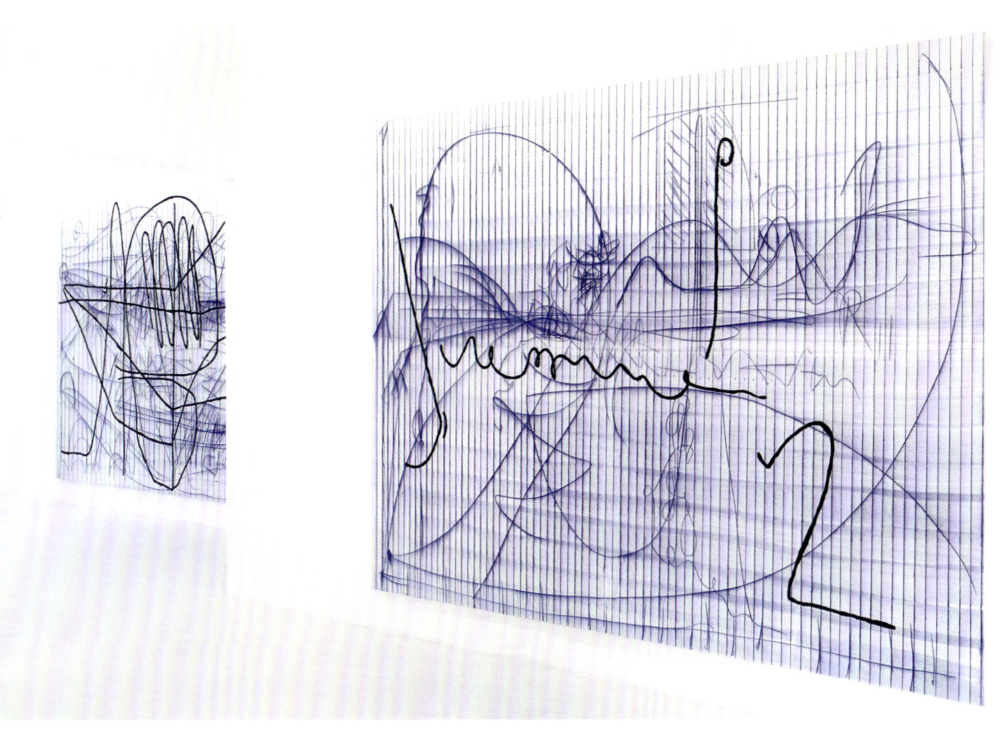

*Spontacts – The Ultra Diagram Series*, Natalia Hug Gallery, Köln / Cologne, 2016

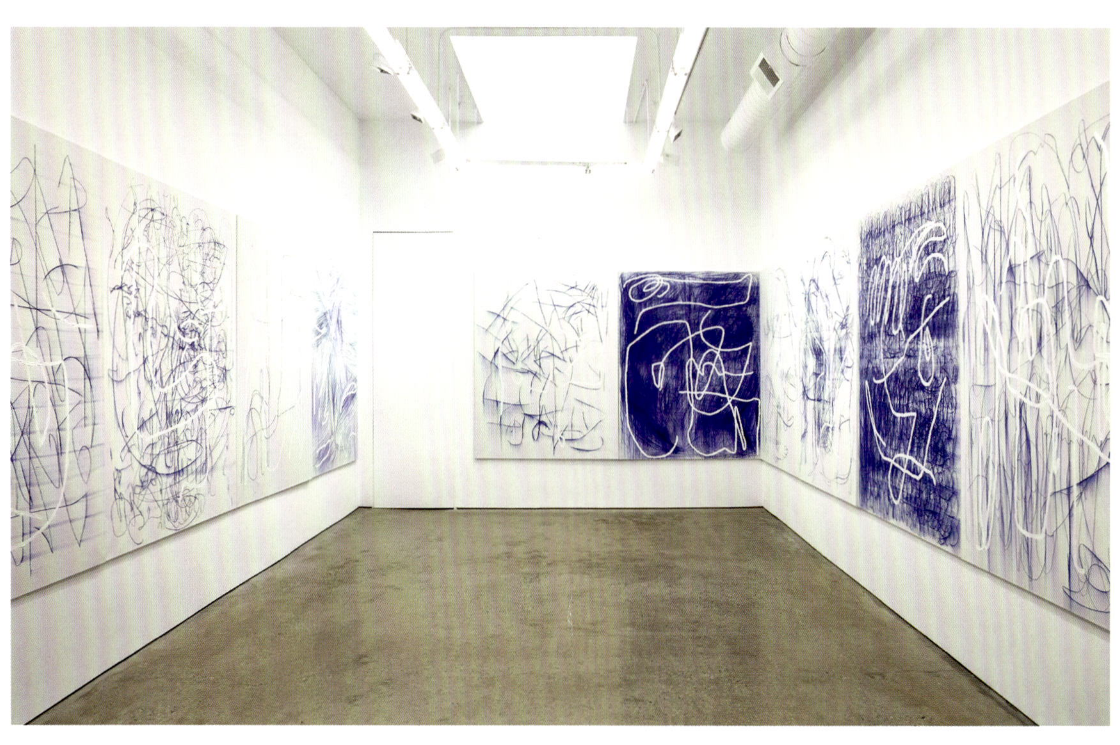

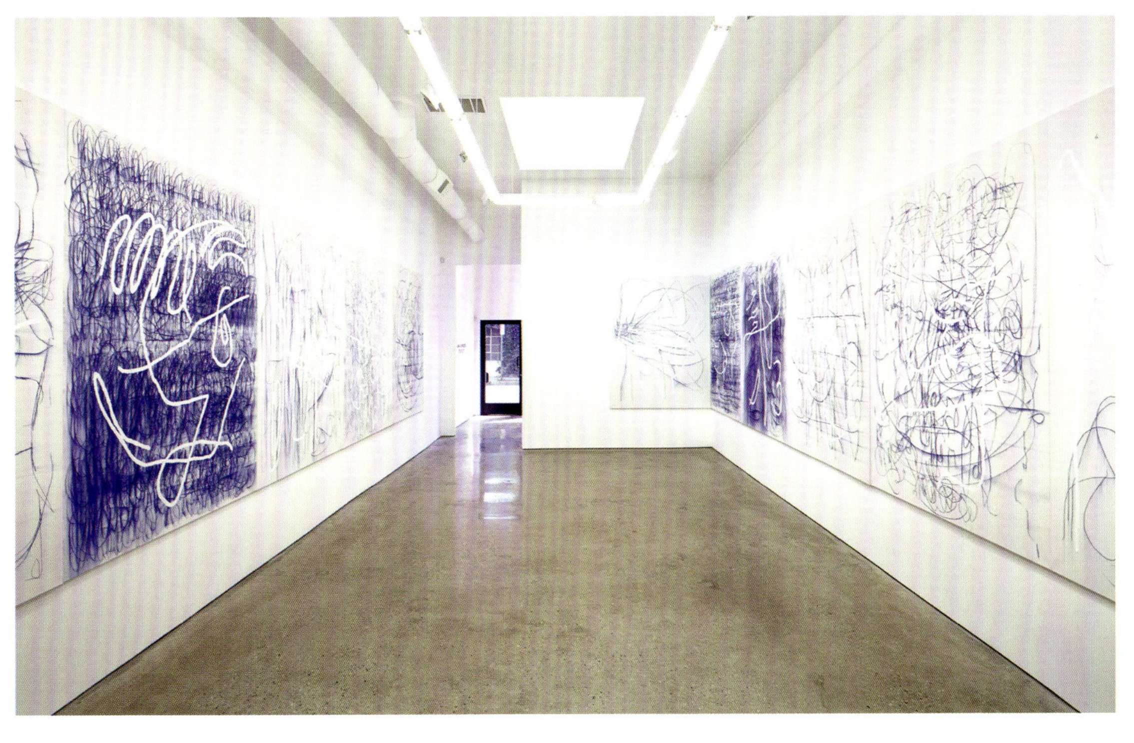

*Spontacts*, Nino Mier Gallery, Los Angeles, 2015

*Herausgeber / Editor*
Kopfermann-Fuhrmann Stiftung,
San-Remo-Straße 6, 40545 Düsseldorf
www.kopfermann-fuhrmann.de

*Autoren / Authors*
Benjamin-Novalis Hofmann, Kuratorium Kopfermann-Fuhrmann Stiftung
Christian Malycha
Jana Schröder

*Übersetzung / Translation*
Amy Klement

*Kurator / Curator*
Benjamin-Novalis Hofmann

*Gestaltung / Design*
Adeline Morlon

*Fotografie / Photography*
Linda Inconi-Jansen
Johannes Bendzulla
Ben Hermanni (Umschlag / Cover)

*Lithografie / Lithography*
bildarbeit Henning Krause



*Gesamtherstellung / Printed by*
Druckerei Kettler, Bönen

*Vertrieb durch / Published by*
Verlag Kettler, Dortmund, www.verlag-kettler.de

Die Deutsche Nationalbibliothek verzeichnet diese Publikation in der Deutschen Nationalbibliografie / The Deutsche Nationalbibliothek lists this publication in the Deutsche Nationalbibliografie: dnb.de.

ISBN 978-3-86206-828-9

Kopfermann-Fuhrmann Stiftung, Düsseldorf 2020